# SCHOLASTIC

**GRADE 5**

# Morning Jumpstarts: Reading

### 100 Independent Practice Pages to Build Essential Skills

Marcia Miller & Martin Lee

New York · Toronto · London · Auckland · Sydney
Mexico City · New Delhi · Hong Kong · Buenos Aires

**Teaching** *Resources*

Edited by Mela Ottaiano

Cover design by Scott Davis

Interior design by Sydney Wright

Interior Illustrations by Teresa Anderko, Paulette Bogan, Steve Cox, Mike Gordon, and James Graham Hale; © 2013 by Scholastic Inc.

Image credits: pages 12, 16, 52 (bottom), 88 (top), 98, and 108 © iStockphoto; pages 20, 28, 34, 52 (top), 88 (bottom), and 96 © Big Stock Photo; pages 36 and 42 © Bettmann/Corbis Images; page 44 © Pierdelune/iStockphoto; page 48 © Everett Collection/Superstock, Inc.; page 84 © Fotosearch/Getty Images; page 102 © Photononstop/Superstock, Inc. All images © 2013.

ISBN: 978-0-545-46424-6

Published by Scholastic Inc.

1 2 3 4 5 6 7 8 9 10    40    20 19 18 17 16 15 14 13

# Contents

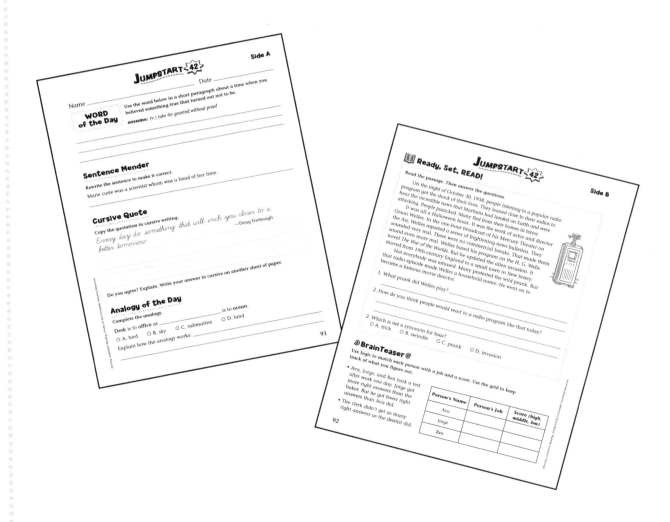

# Introduction

In your busy classroom, you know how vital it is to energize students for the tasks of the day. That's why *Morning Jumpstarts: Reading, Grade 5* is the perfect tool for you.

The activities in this book provide brief and focused individual practice in grade-level skills students are expected to master. Each Jumpstart is a two-page collection of six activities designed to review and reinforce a range of reading and writing skills students will build throughout the year. The consistent format helps students work independently and with confidence. Each Jumpstart includes these features:

- Word of the Day
- Sentence Mender
- Cursive Quote
- Analogy of the Day
- Ready, Set, Read!
- Brainteaser

You can use a Jumpstart in its entirety or, because each feature is self-contained, assign sections at different times of the day or to different groups of learners. The Jumpstart activities will familiarize students with the kinds of challenges they will encounter on standardized tests, and provide a review of skills they need to master. (See page 6 for a close-up look at the features in each Jumpstart.)

The Common Core State Standards (CCSS) for English Language Arts serve as the backbone of the activities in this book. On pages 7–8, you'll find a correlation chart that details how the 50 Jumpstarts dovetail with the widely accepted set of guidelines for preparing students to succeed in reading and language arts.

Generally, we have kept in mind the CCSS "anchor standards" that should inform solid instruction in reading literary and informational texts. In addition, the activity pages provide students with practice in developing and mastering foundational and language skills, summarized below.

ANCHOR STANDARDS
FOR READING
- Key Ideas and Details
- Craft and Structure
- Integration of Knowledge and Ideas
- Range of Reading and Level of Text Complexity

FOUNDATIONAL SKILLS
- Phonics and Word Recognition
- Fluency

LANGUAGE
- Conventions of Standard English
- Knowledge of Language
- Vocabulary Acquisition and Use

*Morning Jumpstarts: Reading, Grade 5* © 2013 Scholastic Teaching Resources

# How to Use This Book

*Morning Jumpstarts: Reading, Grade 5* can be used in many ways—and not just in the morning! You know your students best, so feel free to pick and choose among the activities, and incorporate those you see fit. You can make double-sided copies, or print one side at a time and staple the pages together.

We suggest the following times to present Jumpstarts:
- At the start of the school day, as a way to help students settle into the day's routines.
- Before lunch, as students ready themselves for their midday break.
- After lunch, as a calming transition into the afternoon's plans.
- Toward the end of the day, before students gather their belongings to go home, or for homework.

In general, the Jumpstarts progress in difficulty level and build on skills covered in previous sheets. Preview each one before you assign it, to ensure that students have the skills needed to complete them. Keep in mind, however, that you may opt for some students to skip sections, as appropriate, or complete them together at a later time as part of a small-group or whole-class lesson.

Undoubtedly, students will complete their Jumpstart activity pages at different rates. We suggest that you set up a "what to do when I'm done" plan to give students who need more time a chance to finish without interruption. For example, you might encourage students to complete another Jumpstart. They might also choose to read silently, practice handwriting, journal, or engage in other kinds of writing.

An answer key begins on page 109. You might want to review answers with the whole class. This approach provides opportunities for discussion, comparison, extension, reinforcement, and correlation to other skills and lessons in your current plans. Your observations can direct the kinds of review or reinforcement you may want to add to your lessons. Alternatively, you may find that having students discuss activity solutions and strategies in small groups is another effective approach.

When you introduce the first Jumpstart, walk through its features with your class to provide an overview before you assign it and to make sure students understand the directions. Help students see that the activities in each section focus on different kinds of skills, and let them know that the same sections will repeat throughout each Jumpstart, always in the same order and position. You might want to work through the first few Jumpstarts as a group until students are comfortable with the routine and ready to work independently.

You know best how to assign the work to the students in your class. You might, for instance, stretch a Jumpstart over two days, assigning Side A on the first day and Side B on the second. Although the activities on different Jumpstarts vary in difficulty and in time needed, we anticipate that once students are familiar with the routine, most will be able to complete both sides of a Jumpstart in anywhere from 10 to 20 minutes.

# A Look Inside

Each two-page Jumpstart includes the following skill-building features.

**Word of the Day** The first feature on Side A builds vocabulary. Students read a grade-appropriate word and its definition. A brief writing task asks them to use the new word to demonstrate understanding of its proper usage.

**Sentence Mender** The second Side A feature addresses grade-appropriate conventions of standard English, especially spelling, capitalization, grammar, and punctuation. Students will see a sentence with errors. Their task is to rewrite the sentence correctly. A sample answer is given in the answer key, but it is quite possible that students may devise alternate corrections. Link this task to the revising and proofreading steps of the writing process.

**Cursive Quote** This feature offers students a chance to practice cursive handwriting as they copy and think about a quotation. Students will then write a response to a question that is based on the quote. For this task, direct students to use another sheet of paper, their writing journals, or the back of the Jumpstart sheet if only copied on one side. This section may serve as a springboard for discussion, further study, or correlation with other curriculum areas.

**Analogy of the Day** Every Side A concludes with an analogy that has one missing term. The key is for students to determine the relationship that links the first two words, and then choose the word that will create a second pair of words that relate in the same way. They will also write a description of the relationship. The Jumpstarts present a range of at least a dozen different types of analogies, such as part-whole relationships, object-action, object-description, example-class, antonyms, and so on.

**Ready, Set, Read!** Every Side B begins with a brief reading passage, followed by two or more text-based questions. Passages include fiction and nonfiction, prose and poetry, serious and humorous writing, realistic and fantastical settings. Dig deeper into any passage to inspire discussion, questions, and extension.

Tell students to first read the passage and then answer the questions. If necessary, show them how to fill in the circles for multiple-choice questions. For questions that require student to write, encourage them to use another sheet of paper, if needed.

**Brainteaser** Side B always ends with some form of an entertaining word or language challenge: a puzzle, code, riddle, or other engaging, high-interest task designed to stretch the mind. While some students may find this section particularly challenging, others will relish teasing out tricky solutions. This feature also provides another chance for group work or discussion. It may prove useful to have pairs of students tackle these together. And, when appropriate, invite students to create their own challenges, using ideas sparked by these exercises. Feel free to create your own variations of any brainteasers your class enjoys.

Morning Jumpstarts: Reading, Grade 5 © 2013 Scholastic Teaching Resources

# Connections to the Common Core State Standards

As shown in the chart below and on page 8, the activities in this book will help you meet your specific state reading and language arts standards as well as those outlined in the CCSS. These materials address the following standards for students in grade 5. For details on these standards, visit the CCSS Web site: **www.corestandards.org/the-standards/**.

| JS | 5.RL.1 | 5.RL.2 | 5.RL.3 | 5.RL.4 | 5.RL.5 | 5.RL.6 | 5.RL.7 | 5.RL.10 | 5.RI.1 | 5.RI.2 | 5.RI.3 | 5.RI.4 | 5.RI.7 | 5.RI.8 | 5.RI.10 | 5.RF.3 | 5.RF.4 | 5.L.1 | 5.L.2 | 5.L.3 | 5.L.4 | 5.L.5 | 5.L.6 |
|---|---|---|---|---|---|---|---|---|---|---|---|---|---|---|---|---|---|---|---|---|---|---|---|
| | Reading: Literature | | | | | | | | Reading: Informational Text | | | | | | | Reading: Foundational Skills | | Language | | | | | |
| 1 | • | • | | • | | • | | • | | | | | | | | • | • | • | • | • | • | • | • |
| 2 | | | | | | | | | • | • | • | • | • | • | • | • | • | • | • | • | • | • | • |
| 3 | • | • | • | • | • | • | | • | | | | | | | | • | • | • | • | • | • | • | • |
| 4 | | | | | | | | | • | • | • | • | • | • | • | • | • | • | • | • | • | • | • |
| 5 | | | | | | | | | | • | • | • | | • | • | • | • | • | • | • | • | • | • |
| 6 | | | | | | | | | | • | • | • | • | | • | • | • | • | • | • | • | | • |
| 7 | • | • | • | • | • | • | | • | | | | | | | | • | • | • | • | • | • | • | • |
| 8 | | | | | | | | | • | • | • | • | | • | • | • | • | • | • | • | • | • | • |
| 9 | | | | | | | | | • | • | • | • | | • | • | • | • | • | • | • | • | • | • |
| 10 | | | | | | | | | • | • | • | • | • | • | • | • | • | • | • | • | • | • | • |
| 11 | | • | • | • | | • | | • | | | | | | | | • | • | • | • | • | • | • | • |
| 12 | | | | | | | | | • | • | • | • | • | • | • | • | • | • | • | • | • | • | • |
| 13 | | | | | | | | | • | • | • | • | | • | • | • | • | • | • | • | • | • | • |
| 14 | | | | | | | | | • | • | • | • | • | • | • | • | • | • | • | • | • | | • |
| 15 | | | | | | | | | • | • | • | • | | • | • | • | • | • | • | • | • | | • |
| 16 | | | | | | | | | | • | • | • | | • | • | • | • | • | • | • | • | | • |
| 17 | | | | | | | | | • | • | • | | • | • | • | • | • | • | • | • | • | | • |
| 18 | | | | | | | | | • | • | • | | • | | • | • | • | • | • | • | • | • | • |
| 19 | • | • | | • | | • | | • | | | | | | | | • | • | • | • | • | • | • | • |
| 20 | | | | | | | | | • | • | • | • | • | • | • | • | • | • | • | • | • | • | • |
| 21 | | | | | | | | | • | • | | • | | • | • | • | • | • | • | • | • | | • |
| 22 | | | | | | | | | | • | • | • | | • | • | • | • | • | • | • | • | • | • |
| 23 | | | | | | | | | • | • | • | • | • | | • | • | • | • | • | • | • | • | • |
| 24 | | | | | | | | | • | • | | • | • | • | • | • | • | • | • | • | • | • | • |
| 25 | | | | | | | | | • | • | • | • | | • | • | • | • | • | • | • | • | | • |

# Connections to the Common Core State Standards

| JS | 5.RL.1 | 5.RL.2 | 5.RL.3 | 5.RL.4 | 5.RL.5 | 5.RL.6 | 5.RL.7 | 5.RL.10 | 5.RI.1 | 5.RI.2 | 5.RI.3 | 5.RI.4 | 5.RI.7 | 5.RI.8 | 5.RI.10 | 5.RF.3 | 5.RF.4 | | 5.L.1 | 5.L.2 | 5.L.3 | 5.L.4 | 5.L.5 | 5.L.6 |
|---|---|---|---|---|---|---|---|---|---|---|---|---|---|---|---|---|---|---|---|---|---|---|---|---|
| | Reading: Literature | | | | | | | | Reading: Informational Text | | | | | | | Reading: Foundational Skills | | | Language | | | | | |
| 26 | | | | | | | | | | • | • | • | | | • | • | • | | • | • | • | • | • | • |
| 27 | | | | | | | | | • | • | • | • | | • | • | • | • | | • | • | • | • | • | • |
| 28 | • | • | • | • | | • | | • | | | | | | | | • | • | | • | • | • | • | • | • |
| 29 | | | | | | | | | | • | • | | | • | | • | • | | • | • | • | • | • | • |
| 30 | | | | | | | | | | • | • | • | | | • | • | • | | • | • | • | • | • | • |
| 31 | | | | | | | | | | • | • | • | | • | • | • | • | | • | • | • | • | • | • |
| 32 | | | | | | | | | | • | • | • | | • | • | • | • | | • | • | • | • | • | • |
| 33 | • | • | • | • | • | • | • | • | | | | | | | | | | | • | • | • | • | • | • |
| 34 | | | | | | | | | | • | • | • | | • | • | • | • | | • | • | • | • | • | • |
| 35 | • | • | | • | | • | | • | | | | | | | | • | • | | • | • | • | • | • | • |
| 36 | | | | | | | | | • | • | | • | | • | • | • | • | | • | • | • | • | • | • |
| 37 | | | | | | | | | • | • | • | • | | • | • | • | • | | • | • | • | • | • | • |
| 38 | | | | | | | | | • | • | | • | | • | • | • | • | | • | • | • | • | • | • |
| 39 | • | • | • | • | • | • | • | • | | | | | | | | • | • | | • | • | • | • | • | • |
| 40 | | | | | | | | | • | • | • | • | • | • | • | | | | • | • | • | • | • | • |
| 41 | | | | | | | | | • | • | • | • | | • | • | • | | | • | • | • | • | • | • |
| 42 | | | | | | | | | • | • | • | • | | | • | | | | • | • | • | • | • | • |
| 43 | | | | | | | | | | • | • | | | | • | • | | | • | • | • | • | • | • |
| 44 | | | | | | | | | • | • | • | | | • | | • | | | • | • | • | • | • | • |
| 45 | | | | | | | | | • | • | • | • | | • | | • | | | • | • | • | • | • | • |
| 46 | | • | • | • | | | | • | | | | | | | | • | | | • | • | • | • | • | • |
| 47 | | | | | | | | | • | • | • | • | • | • | • | | • | | • | • | • | • | • | • |
| 48 | | | | | | | | | • | • | | • | | • | • | | • | | • | • | | • | | • |
| 49 | | | | | | | | | • | • | | • | | • | • | | | | • | • | | • | | • |
| 50 | | | | | | | | | • | • | • | • | | • | • | | • | | • | • | • | • | | • |

8

Morning Jumpstarts: Reading, Grade 5 © 2013 Scholastic Teaching Resources

Name _____ Date _____

**WORD of the Day**

Use the word below in a short paragraph about something that stops progress or prevents movement.

**barrier:** (n.) *something that stands in the way; obstacle*

_____

_____

_____

## Sentence Mender

**Rewrite the sentence to make it correct.**

I one furst prize kerry said with pride

_____

## Cursive Quote

**Copy the quotation in cursive writing.**

*Words are the voice of the heart.*

—Confucius

_____

_____

_____

What do you think the philosopher meant? Write your answer in cursive on another sheet of paper.

## Analogy of the Day

**Complete the analogy.**

**Bear** is to **den** as _____ is to **web**.

○ A. house      ○ B. cub      ○ C. search engine      ○ D. spider

Explain how the analogy works: _____

_____

## 📖 Ready, Set, READ!

**Read the story. Then answer the questions.**

Not only is Molly the prettiest dog that ever lived, she's the smartest. I am not talking through my hat. My dog is a genius.

We live in an apartment building, so we can't simply let Molly out into the backyard to do her business. No, we need to put on her leash and take her to a nearby park. Molly understands. To inform us that she needs to go out, she'll whack the bells dangling from our doorknob. Smart to have learned this, right? But yesterday, she outdid herself.

We were eating when Molly trotted over, bringing a sock as a gift. (She's well brought up, you see.) Then she barked. Was it a "play with me" bark? An "I'm thirsty" bark? Who knows? They all sound pretty much alike. When she barked again, I decided to get to the bottom of the matter.

"Molly, if you need to go out, go whack the bells. Stop barking."

Giving me a dismissive look she generally reserves for a cat toy, she padded out of the room and gave those bells a thumping they'll never forget.

So, what do you think? Amazing, right?

1. What does it mean when the writer says he is not *talking through his hat*?

_____

_____

2. Why do you think Molly gave her owner a dismissive look? _____

_____

## ๑ BrainTeaser ๑

Climb the word ladder to change *give* to *take*. Change only one letter at a time. Write the new word on each step.

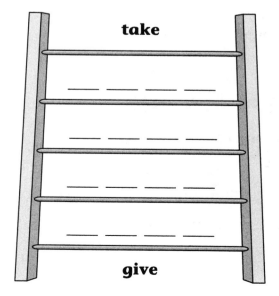

take

give

*Morning Jumpstarts: Reading, Grade 5* © 2013 Scholastic Teaching Resources

Name _____ Date _____

## WORD of the Day

Use the word below in a short paragraph about a hot-tempered person or group.

**aggressive**: (adj.) *taking the first step in a quarrel; forceful*

_____

_____

_____

## Sentence Mender

**Rewrite the sentence to make it correct.**

Jasons brews on he leg caused him to lemp.

_____

## Cursive Quote

**Copy the quotation in cursive writing.**

*A sense of curiosity is nature's original school of education.*

—Dr. Smiley Blanton

_____

_____

_____

**What did Dr. Blanton mean? Write your answer in cursive on another sheet of paper.**

## Analogy of the Day

**Complete the analogy.**

**Big** is to **small** as _____ is to **wet**.

○ A. drenched    ○ B. dry    ○ C. soaked    ○ D. hot

Explain how the analogy works: _____

_____

#  Ready, Set, READ!

**Read the passage. Then answer the questions.**

I like spicy food—the hotter the better! Until recently, I had never tasted a food that was too much for my taste buds. That is, until I came across a Scotch bonnet pepper. This little red bomb nearly set the insides of my mouth on fire! I wish I'd known before I took a curious bite. That's how I learned about Wilbur Scoville.

In 1912, Dr. Scoville was working for a large medicine company. He studied how people perceive flavors, especially the "heat" in spicy things. Scoville devised a way to measure and rank the heat levels of chili peppers. His system used numbers that still bear his name—Scoville units. Bell peppers have a Scoville score of 0. This means that they are not at all hot and spicy. The little Scotch bonnet, on the other hand, scores a whopping 250,000 Scoville units. No wonder my eyeballs spun around in my skull!

1. What does the writer mean by "nearly set the insides of my mouth on fire"?

   _____

   _____

2. Suppose you taste a pepper rated at 50 Scoville units. Describe how you would expect it to taste.

   _____

   _____

# ๑ BrainTeaser ๑

**Use the clues to complete a word that starts with *pat*.**

1. Round, flat piece of meat        P A T ____ ____

2. Fabric to mend a hole            P A T ____ ____

3. Paved area of a house            P A T ____ ____

4. Go around to watch or guard      P A T ____ ____ ____

5. Repeating plan                   P A T ____ ____ ____ ____

6. Sick person in hospital          P A T ____ ____ ____

12

Name _____ Date _____

## WORD of the Day

Use the word below in a short paragraph about horses.

**stampede:** (v.) *make a sudden, wild rush, usually in fear*

_____

_____

_____

## Sentence Mender

Rewrite the sentence to make it correct.

The new glass Building on Spring street sparkels like a dimind.

_____

## Cursive Quote

Copy the quotation in cursive writing.

*Many argue; not many converse.*

—Louisa May Alcott

What does *converse* mean? Write your answer in cursive on another sheet of paper.

## Analogy of the Day

Complete the analogy.

**Sad** is to **frown** as _____ is to **smile**.

○ A. worried     ○ B. annoyed     ○ C. happy     ○ D. awkward

Explain how the analogy works: _____

_____

**Ready, Set, READ!**

**Read the passage. Then answer the questions.**

The brothers arrived in the United States in 1905. Thanks to a single gold coin, they came with a reputation for hard work and honesty.

Mano and Miklos were housepainters. They had a gift for color and an eye for detail. But times were tough and they were poor. That changed when a rich duke bought a big house in town. It needed painting. The duke hired M & M Painters.

While painting a bedroom, Miklos spotted a shiny object wedged between an elegant dresser and the wall. The boys looked at it and at one another. It was a gold coin, worth a year's wages. They were excited, but knew what to do. "We must give it back," Mano said.

Miklos agreed. He went to find the duke. Surprised and pleased, the duke accepted the coin. In return, he gave the brothers food to take to their family. But more significantly, he sang their praises to other wealthy families. He spread the word that the boys were as trustworthy as they were talented.

Business took off. Within a few years, so did the brothers. They crossed the Atlantic with high hopes. Today, Gold Coin Paints is a large company that still prides itself as much on its integrity as on the quality of its products.

1. Why do you think Mano and Miklos returned the coin? _____

_____

2. What does *sang their praises* mean? _____

_____

3. How does this story end? _____

_____

## ⑨ BrainTeaser ⑥

Write the words from the word bank in alphabetical order in the rows of the grid. Circle the column that names *part* of a piece of furniture.

Word Bank

| | |
|---|---|
| SONATA | SORTIE |
| SPIDER | SOBBED |
| SOCCER | SORROW |

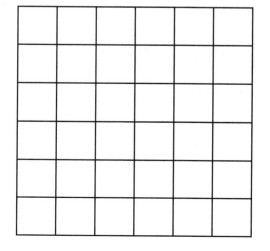

*Morning Jumpstarts: Reading, Grade 5* © 2013 Scholastic Teaching Resources

# JUMPSTART 4

Name _____ Date _____

## WORD of the Day

Use the word below in a short paragraph about a trial.

**verdict:** (n.) *the decision of a jury or a judge; any decision*

_____

_____

_____

## Sentence Mender

**Rewrite the sentence to make it correct.**

We should ask he to seize playing him's drums so late at knight.

_____

## Cursive Quote

**Copy the quotation in cursive writing.**

*Delay is preferable to error.*

—Thomas Jefferson

_____

_____

_____

**Is this good advice? Explain. Write your answer in cursive on another sheet of paper.**

## Analogy of the Day

**Complete the analogy.**

**Lunch** is to **dinner** as _____ is to **evening**.

○ A. afternoon   ○ B. darkness   ○ C. breakfast   ○ D. television

Explain how the analogy works: _____

_____

# 📖 Ready, Set, READ!

**Read the passage. Then answer the questions.**

More than a thousand years ago, when their southern neighbors stayed close to shore, the Norse were the leading sea power in Europe. These intrepid mariners boldly sailed into the Atlantic. They established colonies in Iceland and Greenland. Then one of these Vikings, Leif Erickson, ventured farther west. Soon, coastal birds told him that land was near. He and his crew established a settlement by the shore. He called it Vinland. Like Columbus had 500 years later, Erickson thought he'd arrived in Asia.

In fact, landfall was neither in Japan nor in China, but at the northern tip of Newfoundland. This Canadian spot is known today as L'Anse aux Meadows. The remains of a Norse settlement were discovered there in 1960. Excavations have shown that Vinland was the first European settlement in North America.

But the Norse were hardly the first inhabitants of the region. Indigenous people had been living there successfully for 5,000 years. They wanted no part of their new neighbors. Erickson and his group felt unsafe. They packed up and sailed back to Greenland.

1. Why did the Norse leave Vinland? _____

_____

2. What does *intrepid* mean?
   ○ A. curious    ○ B. fearless    ○ C. skilled    ○ D. adventurous

# 🌀 BrainTeaser 🌀

An *anagram* is a new word made using all the letters of another word. *Tap* is an anagram for *pat*.

**Make an anagram for each word.**

1. acre ⇔ _____    4. react ⇔ _____

2. pest ⇔ _____    5. raspy ⇔ _____

3. baled ⇔ _____   6. poems ⇔ _____

*Morning Jumpstarts: Reading, Grade 5* © 2013 Scholastic Teaching Resources

Name _____ Date _____

## WORD of the Day

Use the word below in a short descriptive paragraph about a photograph.

**vivid**: (adj.) *strikingly bright; brilliant; strong and clear*

_____

_____

_____

## Sentence Mender

**Rewrite the sentence to make it correct.**

The Detroit tigers played a Double Header on labor day.

_____

## Cursive Quote

**Copy the quotation in cursive writing.**

*Those who lose dreaming are lost.*

—Australian proverb

................................................

................................................

................................................

What is the meaning of this proverb? Write your answer in cursive on another sheet of paper.

## Analogy of the Day

**Complete the analogy.**

**Instrument** is to **trombone** as _____ is to **oak**.

○ A. acorn      ○ B. trumpet      ○ C. oatmeal      ○ D. tree

Explain how the analogy works: _____

_____

## Ready, Set, READ!

Read the passage.
Then answer the questions.

How would you like to find a tree that was new to science? Or better still, how would you like to discover a "dinosaur" still living on earth? Well, both those things happened to park ranger David Noble. They happened when he was out hiking in the brush in a national park. This was in New South Wales, Australia. It was September 1994.

A bizarre looking tree with spiraling fernlike yellow-green leaves caught his eye. He had seen nothing like it before. It had multiple trunks. Its bark looked like it was covered in chocolate bubbles. The adventurous ranger had discovered a tree that, before then, had been known only from 200-million-year-old fossil records. But there it was—a wollemia nobilis! And Noble was touching it!

Today there are fewer than 100 of these ancient trees alive in the wild. Thanks to the bush-walking ranger, they are now legally protected.

1. What does it mean that something *caught his eye*?

_____

_____

_____

_____

_____

2. Why was discovering this tree like discovering a dinosaur?

_____

_____

_____

_____

_____

## ⊚ BrainTeaser ⊚

Use the 12 words in the word bank to make a tongue twister. It is a question that begins with *If*. Write your idea below. Then try to say it three times in a row!

| Word Bank | | |
| --- | --- | --- |
| chews | Stu | shoes |
| choose | should | short |
| shoes | chews | Stu |
| short | he | the |

If _____

_____

_____

*Morning Jumpstarts: Reading, Grade 5* © 2013 Scholastic Teaching Resources

Name _____ Date _____

## WORD of the Day

Use the word below in a short paragraph about removing yourself from a competition.

**withdraw:** (v.) *take back or remove*

_____

_____

_____

## Sentence Mender

**Rewrite the sentence to make it correct.**

What is the hieght, in feat, of that ate-story building.

_____

## Cursive Quote

**Copy the quotation in cursive writing.**

*Wonder is the beginning of wisdom.*

—Anonymous

_____

_____

_____

**Do you agree? Explain. Write your answer in cursive on another sheet of paper.**

## Analogy of the Day

**Complete the analogy.**

**Grass** is to **green** as _____ is to **jagged**.

○ A. park      ○ B. knife      ○ C. jar      ○ D. jogged

Explain how the analogy works: _____

_____

**Side B**

# 📖 Ready, Set, READ!

**Read the passage. Then answer the questions.**

Are you a fan of lighthouses? Many people are. These solemn, sturdy structures dot our coastlines. They have long been attractions for visitors as well as beacons for approaching ships.

The world's first lighthouse was built by the Greeks. They built it on Pharos, a small island very near to the port city of Alexandria, Egypt, some 2,300 years ago. Its purpose was to guide merchant ships entering the port. It was constructed also as a symbol of Greek power.

Reaching a height of more than 350 feet, the Pharos lighthouse was for centuries the tallest structure on earth. It had a mirror at its apex that reflected sunlight by day. At night, fires were lit near the top. They could be seen by sailors more than 30 miles out at sea. The structure was famous in its time and is remembered as one of the Seven Wonders of the Ancient World.

Over the years, a series of earthquakes damaged the light-colored stone structure. It had disappeared altogether by 1480.

1. Why was the lighthouse built?
   - ○ A. to warn of earthquakes
   - ○ B. to make fires
   - ○ C. to light ships
   - ○ D. to guide incoming ships

2. Which is true about the Pharos lighthouse?
   - ○ A. It was like other lighthouses.
   - ○ B. It was made of wood.
   - ○ C. It lasted a long time.
   - ○ D. It was poorly constructed.

# ⊚ BrainTeaser ⊚

*Onomatopoeia* is a word that sounds like what it means.

Examples are *buzz, hiss,* and *jingle.*

**Finish each simple sentence with onomatopoeia.**

1. Engines _____.

2. Clocks _____.

3. Fountains _____.

4. Hikers _____.

5. Plates _____.

6. Owls _____.

*Morning Jumpstarts: Reading, Grade 5* © 2013 Scholastic Teaching Resources

Name _____  Date _____

Use the word below in a short paragraph about preparing for a test, making a presentation, or winning a game.

**strategic:** (adj.) *using skillful planning to manage anything*

_____

_____

_____

## Sentence Mender

Rewrite the sentence to make it correct.

The determinned inventer would not conceed defeet.

_____

## Cursive Quote

Copy the quotation in cursive writing.

*Excellence is not an act, it is a habit.*

—Aristotle

What else do you think should be a habit rather than an act? Write your answer in cursive on another sheet of paper.

## Analogy of the Day

Complete the analogy.

**Toe** is to **foot** as _____ is to **house**.

○ A. tree    ○ B. room    ○ C. yard    ○ D. apartment

Explain how the analogy works: _____

_____

## 📖 Ready, Set, READ!

**Read the story. Then answer the questions.**

I had been sound asleep. So the rustling right outside the tent must have been pretty loud. I lay there, listening intently. My heart was pounding so loudly that I thought the intruder would hear it.

Then came an unmistakable thrashing sound. Something rattled and fell. Maybe it was our lantern, which we'd left on the picnic table. I looked to my friends. Jim was snoring away. Greg hadn't budged. What was with them? Another sound—a crash. Then a spine-tingling roar that made me burrow deep down into my bag and zip it up over my head. I was paralyzed with fear. Finally, after what seemed like hours, the noises stopped. Eventually, I fell back asleep.

I awoke the next morning to learn that I alone heard the rumpus. "Have some eggs, Pete," Greg said, groggily.

"Amazing," Jim added, "that although we left all our food out, nothing was disturbed. No bears around here, I guess."

"Nothing disturbed?" I asked.

"Nothing but our rest," Greg added. "You were chattering away in your sleep all night. Kept us both wide awake."

1. What is a *rumpus*? _____

_____

2. What actually happened during the night? _____

_____

## ☺ BrainTeaser ☺

A *palindrome* is a word that reads the same forward and backward.

**Write a palindrome for each clue.**

1. Even and flat _____.

2. Male and female _____.

3. Look to for information _____.

4. More bloodlike in color _____.

5. Songs for one singer _____.

22

Name _____ Date _____

Use the word below in a short paragraph about an observation.

**apparent**: (adj.) *easy to see or understand; appearing to be*

_____

_____

_____

## Sentence Mender

**Rewrite the sentence to make it correct.**

H'es the older and bigger of the three brother.

_____

## Cursive Quote

**Copy the quotation in cursive writing.**

*Nothing is so burdensome as a secret.*

—French proverb

Do you think this is true? Write your answer in cursive on another sheet of paper.

## Analogy of the Day

**Complete the analogy.**

**Sailor** is to **navy** as _____ is to **class**.

○ A. soldier  ○ B. room  ○ C. school  ○ D. student

Explain how the analogy works: _____

_____

# 📖 Ready, Set, READ!

**Read the passage. Then answer the questions.**

The idea of space vacations has long excited us. Trips to orbiting hotels or holidays on the moon are not new ideas. Science fiction writer Jules Verne wrote about family trips to the moon in the 1860s. By the 1950s, futurists were predicting that American families would be enjoying moon trips by the early 21st century. The airline Pan Am even had a moon-trip waiting list 50 years ago. Really? Yes! And hold onto your hats. They were on to something!

Space travel for fun is here and companies offering it are growing in number. But cheap it is not. A recreational flight to the International Space Station will set you back about $20 million. A little too costly, you say? Well, cheer up. For a measly $200,000, you'll soon be able to take a suborbital flight instead. On one of these, you'll go about 250 miles up in space and enjoy maybe five minutes of weightlessness. And you'll see amazing views of our planet.

So, hurry up and save your pennies. Get your name on a waiting list for a trip that will be out of this world!

1. What choices do you now have for a space vacation?

_____

_____

_____

_____

_____

_____

2. What does the writer imply about costs by using the term "measly" to describe costs?

_____

_____

_____

_____

_____

_____

# 🌀 BrainTeaser 🌀

*Hink Pinks* are one-syllable word pairs that rhyme to fit clues. **Solve these Hink Pink riddles.**

Example
unhappy father =
sad dad

1. What is a cloudy 24 hours? _____

2. What is a sack for *Old Glory*? _____

3. What is a defect in a talon? _____

4. Where do you store a sweeper? _____

5. What is a scary moment on a jet? _____

*Morning Jumpstarts: Reading, Grade 5* © 2013 Scholastic Teaching Resources

Name _____ Date _____

## WORD of the Day

Use the word below in a short paragraph about a painting.

**duplicate:** (v.) *make an exact copy of something or repeat exactly*

_____

_____

_____

## Sentence Mender

**Rewrite the sentence to make it correct.**

The Park Ranjer lead us on the dissent from the mountin.

_____

## Cursive Quote

**Copy the quotation in cursive writing.**

*Bad is never good until worse happens.*

—Danish proverb

_____

_____

_____

Share an experience that proved this proverb to be true. Write it in cursive on another sheet of paper.

## Analogy of the Day

**Complete the analogy.**

**Clean** is to **spotless** as _____ is to **beautiful**.

○ A. nature      ○ B. vacuum      ○ C. pretty      ○ D. gorgeous

Explain how the analogy works: _____

_____

## 📖 Ready, Set, READ!

**Read the passage. Then answer the questions.**

It was explored by Lewis and Clark. It was made famous by Mark Twain. It has been home to riverboats, trade, and gamblers. Towns along it were take-off points for wagon trains going west. Controlling it was key to the North's victory in the Civil War. It is the Mississippi River. And it is the most important and most famous waterway in North America. Every mile of it lies within the United States.

It passes through or borders ten states. At least 3,745 miles long, the Mississippi and its several feeders form one of the longest river systems in the world. That system reaches to the Rocky Mountains to the west and to the Appalachians to the east. To the north, the starting point is in northern Minnesota, near to the Canadian border. It flows by several large cities before it drains into the Gulf of Mexico to the south.

Dozens of bridges span the river. The first was built in 1855. A year later, the first railroad bridge was completed. But a riverboat accidentally rammed into it. The railroad bridge was set afire and destroyed. There was a big lawsuit. The railroad company won the case. Its attorney was a little known country lawyer. That lawyer went on to become America's 16th president.

1. Based on the passage, what do you think a *feeder* is? _____

_____

2. How can you best describe the Mississippi River? _____

_____

## 🎜 BrainTeaser 🎝

*Hinky Pinkies* are two-syllable word pairs that rhyme to fit clues.
**Solve these Hinky Pinky riddles.**

Example
Arctic tooth = polar molar

1. Who packages wafers? _____

2. What moral tale is set in a horse farm? _____

3. What can you call flexible logs? _____

4. Who looks after animals? _____

5. Who captains a sailing ship? _____

Name _____ Date _____

## WORD of the Day

Use the word below in a short paragraph about a letter, photograph, or map that shows something to be true.

**document:** (n.) *something written or an image that gives information or proof*

_____

_____

_____

## Sentence Mender

**Rewrite the sentence to make it correct.**

Dan and iris went to paris to take a french cookin Class.

_____

## Cursive Quote

**Copy the quotation in cursive writing.**

*What is reading but silent conversation?*

—Walter Savage Landon

_____

_____

_____

What do you think Landon meant by this? Write your answer in cursive on another sheet of paper.

## Analogy of the Day

**Complete the analogy.**

**Cry** is to **laugh** as _____ is to **down**.

○ A. whimper      ○ B. up      ○ C. floor      ○ D. high

Explain how the analogy works: _____

_____

## Ready, Set, READ!

**Read the passage. Then answer the questions.**

Have you ever seen tap dancing? The dancers use sounds their shoes make when the metal "taps" on the heels and toes hit the floor. Tap dancing got its start when West African circular dancing got mixed with English clogging and Irish jigs. Over time, tap has become a uniquely American dance form.

The happy marriage of jig and "juba" came about under sad circumstances—on slave ships crossing the Atlantic. Often, the slaves were called on deck to dance. Conditions below were horrible. So the slaves who were forced to dance for their captors were the lucky ones. They got some much-needed fresh air and exercise. On deck, they danced to the sounds of fiddles and bagpipes. As they did, they drew upon the rhythms of their own tribal dances. They combined those steps with the wooden-shoe dancing the sailors enjoyed.

Tap dance continued in America on the plantations. Slaves danced on upturned buckets and on barrel tops. Their style developed and spread. By the late 1800s, tap had become a popular stage dance. Performers today continue to keep this exciting dance form alive.

1. What does the writer mean by *a happy marriage* of the dances?

   _____

   _____

2. What do you think *juba* is? _____

   _____

## ⑨ BrainTeaser ⑥

Unscramble each word.
Write it correctly in the spaces.
Unscramble the boxed letters to
name an African animal.

_____

DENLB   [ ] ___ ___ ___ ___

FETTH   ___ [ ] ___ ___ ___

RHAYI   ___ [ ] ___ ___ ___

ZEAMA   ___ ___ ___ [ ] ___

DOBOR   ___ [ ] ___ ___ ___

*Morning Jumpstarts: Reading, Grade 5 © 2013 Scholastic Teaching Resources*

Name _____ Date _____

## WORD of the Day

Use the word below in a short paragraph about being respectful toward others.

**courteous:** (adj.) *polite and showing respect; considerate*

_____

_____

_____

## Sentence Mender

**Rewrite the sentence to make it correct.**

Us visited south Carolinas first light house.

_____

## Cursive Quote

**Copy the quotation in cursive writing.**

*The wastebasket is a writer's best friend.*

—Isaac Bashevis Singer

**What did Singer mean by this? Write your answer in cursive on another sheet of paper.**

## Analogy of the Day

**Complete the analogy.**

**Clock** is to **tick** as _____ is to **fly**.

○ A. helicopter    ○ B. wing    ○ C. swatter    ○ D. paper

Explain how the analogy works: _____

_____

#  Ready, Set, READ!

**Read the story. Then answer the questions.**

It was the culminating event of the summer: the huge relay race. There were two competing teams, one blue and one white. And there were two of us, me and Larry G., standing at the dock, awaiting the rowboats coming with our painted softballs. Our task: receive our team ball, race across a field, enter the thick woods, make a basket in the court beyond, and then return to the dock and finish line.

My teammate, Buddy, rowed feverishly. But he fell behind. I watched anxiously as Larry got his ball and sped off. By the time Buddy climbed ashore, Larry was into the woods. I ran like the wind after him.

When I reached the court, there was no Larry. Then I spotted him out of the corner of my eye. He was frantically searching the brush for his ball. He must have badly missed his attempt and was suffering the consequences. I like Larry, and thought for a moment about helping. But, naaah! Instead, I took my shot. Luckily, I made the basket on the first try. I gleefully galloped back to the finish line! We won, and I was superhero for a day.

1. Why was the storyteller waiting for Buddy?
   - O A. He missed him.
   - O B. He had to give Buddy a ball.
   - O C. Buddy was bringing the ball.
   - O D. Buddy was late.

2. Where does this story take place?
   - O A. at a summer camp
   - O B. in a basketball arena
   - O C. on a farm
   - O D. in a city

## ☺ BrainTeaser ☺ The word bank lists castle words. Each word is hidden in the puzzle. Find and circle each word.

| Word Bank | |
|---|---|
| BAILEY | PARAPET |
| BARBICAN | PORTCULLIS |
| BATTLEMENT | RAMPART |
| DRAWBRIDGE | SPUR |
| GATEHOUSE | TOWER |
| LOOP | TURRET |
| MOAT | VAULT |
| PANTRY | WALK |

```
P B A T T L E M E N T M P O R
A A S L U X B A R B I C A N A
R I P O R T C U L L I S N M M
A L U O R O K N V A U L T O P
P E R P E W A L K R O Y R A A
E Y G A T E H O U S E J Y T R
T P H U D R A W B R I D G E T
```

*Morning Jumpstarts: Reading, Grade 5* © 2013 Scholastic Teaching Resources

Name _____  Date _____

## WORD of the Day

Use the word below in a short paragraph about a time you did something you were or were not proud of.

**exhibit:** (v.) *show clearly; reveal; to put on display*

_____

_____

_____

## Sentence Mender

**Rewrite the sentence to make it correct.**

This mourning, I had breckfist in my pajomas and split orange juice on it.

_____

## Cursive Quote

**Copy the quotation in cursive writing.**

*Quarrels end, but words once spoken never die.*

—African proverb

_____

_____

_____

**Do you agree? Explain. Write your answer in cursive on another sheet of paper.**

## Analogy of the Day

**Complete the analogy.**

**Apple** is to **fruit** as _____ is to **clothing**.

○ A. shirt    ○ B. store    ○ C. shopper    ○ D. peach

Explain how the analogy works: _____

_____

# 📖 Ready, Set, READ!

**Read the passage. Then answer the questions.**

People once thought that when Europeans reached the Americas they found lands that were thinly populated. They believed that the explorers had discovered a new world. But we now know that this was not so. To see why, take a drive 15 minutes east from St. Louis.

There you'll come upon 120 large mounds. These are the remains of a big settlement that was inhabited for seven centuries. It is called Cahokia. And it had a population of thirty thousand 240 years before Columbus set sail. Cahokia was bigger than London was at that time!

But by 1400, Cahokia was empty. Maybe climate change or poor crops made the people leave. Perhaps war or disease was to blame. We do not yet know. We also don't know where its people went or what tribes they became. But we know Cahokia was there.

Today, Cahokia is a World Heritage Site. It is protected because of how important it is to our understanding of the history of our continent.

1. What did many people used to think about pre-Columbian North America?

_____

_____

_____

_____

_____

_____

2. What does the discovery of Cahokia tell us?

_____

_____

_____

_____

_____

# 🌀 BrainTeaser 🌀

Write a synonym from the word bank for each boldface word below.

1. **grieve** for _____

2. **exclude** from _____

3. **identical** twins _____

4. **justify** the plan _____

5. reckless **assault** _____

6. **neutral** position _____

7. powerful **obstacle** _____

**Word Bank**

attack
barrier
duplicate
impartial
mourn
omit
support

32

Name _____   Date _____

## WORD of the Day

Use the word below in a short paragraph about a time you did the right thing or witnessed someone else doing so.

**moral:** (adj.) *good in character and conduct; just; right*

_____

_____

_____

## Sentence Mender

Rewrite the sentence to make it correct.

Waht should we doe about the worrysome leek in the kichen?

_____

## Cursive Quote

Copy the quotation in cursive writing.

*Kindness, like a boomerang, always returns.*

—Author unknown

What do you think the author meant by this? Write your answer in cursive on another sheet of paper.

## Analogy of the Day

Complete the analogy.

**Dessert** is to **tasty** as _____ is to **sticky**.

○ A. soup      ○ B. tack      ○ C. cookie      ○ D. glue

Explain how the analogy works: _____

_____

## 📖 Ready, Set, READ!

**Read the passage. Then answer the questions.**

In the high desert of Peru there exists a series of designs formed in the ground. Some are just straight lines. Others are geometric shapes. Still others are trees and flowers. There is an assortment of animals, too—giant birds, fish, monkeys, lizards, and llamas. They are huge. The biggest are nearly 700 feet long.

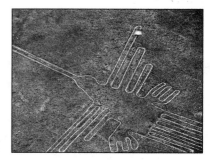

People of the Nazca culture made these enormous shallow shapes maybe 1,500 years ago. To form them, they scraped off a ground cover of reddish pebbles to expose the gray-white ground underneath. Archeologists believe that the Nazca made these figures for religious purposes. They think that these designs were made to be seen by the Nazca gods. This was not so unusual. For instance, the great earthworks of Stonehenge in England were built for the same purpose.

You can see the Nazca lines from surrounding hilltops. But for the best view, you can't beat hopping on an airplane and looking down.

1. What were formed on the ground in the high Peruvian desert?

_____

_____

2. Why were they built? _____

_____

## ☺ BrainTeaser ☺

**Each sentence below has two blanks. Both use the same letters to form two different words. Fill them in. The first one is done for you.**

1. We ___opt___ for a large ___pot___ of ginger tea.

2. I love the cold, but I truly _____ the _____ .

3. The doors of the four _____ must be tightly _____ .

4. Let's have a foot _____ around the one-_____ field.

5. I _____ that she always _____ her glasses at home.

Morning Jumpstarts: Reading, Grade 5 © 2013 Scholastic Teaching Resources

Name _____  Date _____

## WORD of the Day

Use the word below in a short paragraph about a dependable person or machine.

**reliable:** (adj.) *able to be depended upon; trustworthy*

_____

_____

_____

## Sentence Mender

**Rewrite the sentence to make it correct.**

The number has too sixs and three fores.

_____

## Cursive Quote

**Copy the quotation in cursive writing.**

*The quieter you become, the more you can hear.*

—Ram Dass

_____

_____

_____

**Is this good advice? Explain. Write your answer in cursive on another sheet of paper.**

## Analogy of the Day

**Complete the analogy.**

**Car** is to **garage** as _____ is to **hangar**.

○ A. clothing    ○ B. airplane    ○ C. closet    ○ D. parking

Explain how the analogy works: _____

_____

## 📖 Ready, Set, READ!

**Read the passage. Then answer the questions.**

The statement *there's a sucker born every minute* came first from a famous hoax. The hoax was the work of George Hull. He fooled thousands of people.

In the 1860s, Hull hired men to carve out a large block of gypsum. Then he hired someone to form from it a ten-foot man. Next, he hired someone else to use chemicals to make the figure look human and very old. Then he had the figure shipped to Cardiff, New York, where a team buried it behind the barn on William Newell's farm. Lastly, Hull hired another crew to "accidentally" come upon the giant while digging a well.

Newell, Hull's cousin, made the most of this great "discovery" on his land. He charged 25¢ to see his amazing old man. Then he doubled his price. Scientists quickly proclaimed the Cardiff Giant a fake. Nonetheless, people continued to fork over money to see it wherever it was exhibited. Newell sold his man and made a fortune. Before too long, Americans were treated to a series of similar hoaxes.

**THE GREAT**
## CARDIFF GIANT!
Discovered at Cardiff, Onondaga Co., N. Y., is now on Exhibition in the
### Geological Hall, Albany,
For a few days only.
**HIS DIMENSIONS.**

Length of Body, — — 10 feet, 4 1-2 inches.
Length of Head from Chin to Top of Head, 21
Length of Nose, — — — 6
Across the Nostrils, — — 3 1-2
Width of Mouth, — — — 5
Circumference of Neck, — — 37
Shoulders, from point to point, 3 feet, 1 1-2
Length of Right Arm, — 4 feet, 9 1-2
Across the Wrist, — — — 5
Across the Palm of Hand, — — 7
Length of Second Finger, — — 8
Around the Thighs, — 6 feet, 3 1-2
Diameter of the Thigh, — — 13
Through the Calf of Leg, — — 9 1-2
Length of Foot, — — — 21
Across the Ball of Foot, — — 8
Weight, — — — 2990 pounds.
ALBANY, November 20th, 1869.

A poster from 1869

1. What was buried behind Newell's barn? _____

_____

2. Explain the meaning of the italicized statement in the first sentence.

_____

_____

## ☾ BrainTeaser ☾

Put a ✓ in the box to show whether the word names one thing or more than one. If you can't tell, ✓ the last box.

| Word | 1 thing | 2 or more | Can't tell |
|---|---|---|---|
| 1. furniture | | | |
| 2. aircraft | | | |
| 3. oxen | | | |
| 4. moose | | | |
| 5. dice | | | |
| 6. cactus | | | |
| 7. people | | | |

Morning Jumpstarts: Reading, Grade 5 © 2013 Scholastic Teaching Resources

Name _____  Date _____

**WORD of the Day**

Use the word below in a short paragraph about a time you or another messed up something that had to be done.

**bungle:** (v.) *do or make something in a clumsy, unskilled way*

_____

_____

_____

## Sentence Mender

**Rewrite the sentence to make it correct.**

Megs teacher and her mom agrees that Meg handwrite is eligible

_____

## Cursive Quote

**Copy the quotation in cursive writing.**

*Goals are the fuel in the furnace of achievement.*

—Brian Tracy

_____

_____

Explain what this means in your own words. Write your explanation in cursive on another sheet of paper.

## Analogy of the Day

**Complete the analogy.**

**Tornado** is to **destruction** as _____ is to **learn**.

○ A. study     ○ B. work     ○ C. hurricane     ○ D. forget

Explain how the analogy works: _____

_____

# Ready, Set, READ!

**Read the passage. Then answer the questions.**

When Jean Craighead George was in kindergarten she got her first pet—a turkey vulture. This is not as unusual as it sounds. Her family loved animals of all kinds. Her father worked as a scientist for the U. S. Forest Service. Her two brothers both grew up to study bears.

When Jean grew up, she became an author of children's books. She wrote more than 100 of them. It makes sense that she would write about the rugged wilderness and its hardy inhabitants. In *My Side of the Mountain*, a young boy survives on his own in the mountains of New York State. In *Juliet of the Wolves*, a 13-year-old girl befriends a pack of wolves. The pack helps her survive in the challenging wilds of Alaska. In 1973, Jean won a prized Newbery Medal, the highest honor given to writers of children's books.

Along with her husband, John George, Jean kept up a love of wildlife and wild animals. Their household was a zoo with its beavers, owls, crows, and dozens and dozens of dogs and cats.

1. What did Jean Craighead George write about?

_____

_____

2. What might explain her love of animals and nature?

_____

_____

# ☺ BrainTeaser ☺

Write *a*, *e*, *i*, *o*, *u*, or *y* to finish spelling each state.

1. T ____ x ____ s

2. V ____ rm ____ nt

3. K ____ nt ____ ck ____

4. N ____ br ____ sk ____

5. W ____ sc ____ ns ____ n

6. D ____ l ____ w ____ r ____

7. M ____ r ____ l ____ nd

8. Fl ____ r ____ d ____

9. K ____ ns ____ s

10. M ____ nt ____ n ____

*Morning Jumpstarts: Reading, Grade 5* © 2013 Scholastic Teaching Resources

Name _____ Date _____

```
┌─────────────────┐
│ WORD            │
│ of the Day      │
└─────────────────┘
```

Use the word below in a short paragraph about witnessing an avalanche.

**avalanche:** (n.) *large mass of snow or rocks that suddenly slides down a mountain; anything like this event*

_____

_____

_____

## Sentence Mender

**Rewrite the sentence to make it correct.**

It is easiest to put an bridal on a horse then on a mewl?

_____

## Cursive Quote

**Copy the quotation in cursive writing.**

*Comedy is simply a funny way of being serious.*

—Peter Ustinov

_____

_____

_____

**What did Ustinov mean by this? Write your answer in cursive on another sheet of paper.**

## Analogy of the Day

**Complete the analogy.**

**Drawer** is to **dresser** as _____ is to **mug.**

○ A. closet    ○ B. pug    ○ C. cup    ○ D. handle

Explain how the analogy works: _____

_____

 # Ready, Set, READ!

**Read the passage. Then answer the questions.**

If you ask someone what a calorie is, you are likely to get a confused answer. "It's a thing in food that makes you fat," someone might reply. Although calorie is a word we might hear every day, its meaning is a mystery to many.

A calorie is actually the amount of energy it takes to raise the temperature of a gram of water about 1° Celsius. The key word in this definition is energy. Calories are fuel. They are to our bodies what gas is to a car. We need calories. If we don't take in enough of them, our brain, heart, and lungs won't work as well as they can.

People need a certain number of calories daily to function well. If people eat foods with too many calories, they will most likely gain weight. If they take in too few calories, they will probably lose weight. The best idea is to eat moderately and healthfully to stay strong and fit.

1. What is the most important thing to know about calories?
   - ○ A. They should be avoided.
   - ○ B. They are a gas.
   - ○ C. They measure energy.
   - ○ D. They are mysterious.

2. Why do we need calories?
   - ○ A. to fuel our bodies
   - ○ B. to gain weight
   - ○ C. to stop being hungry
   - ○ D. to raise our temperature

# ⊙ BrainTeaser ⊙

Complete the category chart. The letters above each column tell the first letter for each word. One word is done for you.

|  | F | A | C | T |
|---|---|---|---|---|
| **Cars** |  |  |  |  |
| **Colors** |  |  | cobalt |  |
| **Foods** |  |  |  |  |
| **Languages** |  |  |  |  |

*Morning Jumpstarts: Reading, Grade 5* © 2013 Scholastic Teaching Resources

Name _____     Date _____

## WORD of the Day

Use the word below in a short paragraph about a time you had to be particularly careful.

**cautious**: (adj.) *very careful to avoid risks or mistakes*

_____

_____

_____

## Sentence Mender

**Rewrite the sentence to make it correct.**

The track teems captian can run like a dear.

_____

## Cursive Quote

**Copy the quotation in cursive writing.**

*Children have more need of models than critics.*

—Carolyn Coats

_____

_____

**What did Coats advise about how best to guide children? Write your answer in cursive on another sheet of paper.**

## Analogy of the Day

**Complete the analogy.**

**Athlete** is to **team** as _____ is to **crew**.

○ A. owner      ○ B. boat      ○ C. stadium      ○ D. co-pilot

Explain how the analogy works: _____

_____

# 📖 Ready, Set, READ!

**Read the passage. Then answer the questions.**

Lewis and Clark are the most famous American explorers. Their efforts resulted in a wealth of information about the land, rivers, and people of the West. But the achievements of those two bold adventurers were dwarfed by those of naval officer Charles Wilkes.

Wilkes led what came to be called the Wilkes Expedition. During four years of wandering that began in 1838, his six ships carrying 346 men sailed around the globe. His task was to map the entire Pacific Ocean. He did that and more. He found that some islands thought to exist did not. And he discovered several new ones. His ships had scientists and artists on board. They gathered and recorded data that greatly increased what was then known about our world.

Wilkes' key discovery was a continent. Others before him had spotted parts of Antarctica. But Wilkes skirted the coastline for more than 1,500 miles. He found that it was continuous and not just a string of islands. He gave it its name. Charles Wilkes never received the fame Lewis and Clark did. But he should have.

1. What was the Wilkes Expedition's task? _____

_____

2. Why does Wilkes deserve the fame Lewis and Clark got?

_____

_____

# ꩜ BrainTeaser ꩜

Unscramble the words so that all rhyme.

1. OZO _____

2. UOY _____

3. UTUT _____

4. KWEN _____

5. ECUL _____

6. HOES _____

7. EWIV _____

8. PEUR _____

*Morning Jumpstarts: Reading, Grade 5* © 2013 Scholastic Teaching Resources

Name _____ Date _____

## WORD of the Day

Use the word below in a short paragraph about something you think we should protect from change.

**preserve**: (v.) *keep something from harm or change; to keep food from spoiling*

_____

_____

_____

## Sentence Mender

Rewrite the sentence to make it correct.

That wonderfull dog gracie is the apple of her owner's nose.

_____

## Cursive Quote

Copy the quotation in cursive writing.

*A writer only begins a book. A reader finishes it.*

—Samuel Johnson

What did Johnson mean by this? Do you agree? Write your answer in cursive on another sheet of paper.

## Analogy of the Day

Complete the analogy.

**Cow** is to **moo** as _____ is to **ring**.

○ A. circus      ○ B. bell      ○ C. bull      ○ D. finger

Explain how the analogy works: _____

_____

 # Ready, Set, READ!

**Read the passage. Then answer the questions.**

General Sherman, the man, was a famous soldier. General Sherman, the tree, is the largest on earth. It was named by a cavalry officer who served under Sherman. The 2,700-year-old giant tree lives in California's Sequoia National Park. It is nearly 275 feet tall. The distance around its huge trunk is about 103 feet.

GENERAL SHERMAN

This is one large tree. But it is not the world's tallest. That honor goes to the Hyperion Tree. It is a coastal redwood, also in California, that is 105 feet taller. Nor is it the widest tree. A tropical South African baobab has a circumference that tops 154 feet.

It is not the oldest tree, either. Compared to Methuselah, it is a youngster. That ancient pine is more than 4,800 years old. And Methuselah became number one only after Prometheus was cut down in 1964. That Nevada senior citizen was about 5,000 years old when it met its end.

1. About how much older than General Sherman is Methuselah?

_____

2. How tall is the Hyperion Tree? _____

_____

3. What does *circumference* mean? _____

_____

# ☺ BrainTeaser ☺

Write all the different words you can spell using three or more letters from the word *consideration.*

_____

_____

_____

_____

Name _____ Date _____

## WORD of the Day

Use the word below in a short paragraph about a famous ruler of a kingdom or empire.

**monarch:** (n.) *a king, queen, emperor or other ruler*

_____

_____

_____

## Sentence Mender

Rewrite the sentence to make it correct.

Many cabel customers have finded the new servic to be worser than it were before.

_____

## Cursive Quote

Copy the quotation in cursive writing.

*The best way to predict your future is to create it.*

—Unknown

_____

_____

_____

What did the author mean by this advice? Write your answer in cursive on another sheet of paper.

## Analogy of the Day

Complete the analogy.

**Airplane** is to **travel** as _____ is to **drink**.

○ A. water     ○ B. car     ○ C. straw     ○ D. eat

Explain how the analogy works: _____

_____

## 📖 Ready, Set, READ!

**Read the story. Then answer the questions.**

The old jail was the first building I explored. In fact, there were only a couple of others still standing, each a shell of what it used to be. When the mine went bust, everyone left, their hopes dashed. None came back.

I left my coat and camera on a bench in the cell and went to see what remained of the town. There wasn't much but I saw it all, including the schoolhouse and the open mine. Then I got back in the car and drove off to find a place to sleep that night.

At the motel I remembered what I'd left back in the ghost town. Darn! The next morning I took the long drive back. I parked and then ducked into the jail. There was my jacket. Oddly, it was now hanging from a nail. The camera was gone. My jacket felt heavy when I retrieved it. So I reached into the pockets. I found within them a worn deck of cards and a tarnished sheriff's star. And there, too, was a handkerchief with an inscription. It read *Forever Yours, Bess*. I stood there with my mouth agape.

1. Where was the writer of this story visiting? _____

    _____

2. What do you think happened in that jail? _____

    _____

3. What does *agape* mean? _____

    _____

## ☺ BrainTeaser ☺

Each word group below can form a sentence, but only if you put the words in a sensible order. Start each sentence with a capital letter. Use an end mark.

1. door the garage close _____

2. trust how a can liar you _____

3. oysters noisy annoy noises _____

4. yet eaten they lunch haven't _____

5. to Spanish learning are speak you _____

*Morning Jumpstarts: Reading, Grade 5* © 2013 Scholastic Teaching Resources

Name _____ Date _____

### WORD of the Day

Use the word below in a short paragraph about something you wish you could easily carry around with you.

**portable:** (adj.) *able to be carried or moved; easily carried*

_____

_____

_____

## Sentence Mender

**Rewrite the sentence to make it correct.**

Erin was upsit when she had been learning that she could'nt go with her friends.

_____

## Cursive Quote

**Copy the quotation in cursive writing.**

*To ease another's heartache is to forget one's own.*

—Abraham Lincoln

_____

_____

_____

**Do you think this is true? Tell why. Write your answer in cursive on another sheet of paper.**

## Analogy of the Day

**Complete the analogy.**

**Ice** is to **cold** as _____ is to **blue**.

○ A. snow     ○ B. sky     ○ C. steam     ○ D. green

Explain how the analogy works: _____

_____

## 📖 Ready, Set, READ!

**Read the passage. Then answer the questions.**

You'll agree that in a democracy all citizens should have the right to vote. But for years, only white males could vote in the United States. This has changed, as you know. We owe thanks for this in large part to the tireless work of Susan B. Anthony and Elizabeth Cady Stanton. They were two of the leaders of the women's movement of the 19th and early 20th centuries.

Anthony and Stanton worked to get equal rights for women. They gave speeches and wrote articles. But fairness for women in jobs, in pay, and in property disputes did not come easily. It was an uphill battle. Getting women the right to vote was a big part of that fight.

Both Anthony and Stanton kept up the struggle. Neither lived to see women finally go to the polls. But that day wouldn't have come without them and those who followed their lead. The efforts of those brave American citizens show that determined people working together can be a powerful force for change.

1. Who were Susan B. Anthony and Elizabeth Cady Stanton? _____

_____

2. Why do you think the writer describes the women's movement as an uphill battle?

_____

_____

## 🌀 BrainTeaser 🌀

**Use each clue to complete a word that starts with *ten*.**

1. Camping shelter      T E N ___

2. One of ten equal parts   T E N ___ ___

3. Singing voice      T E N ___ ___

4. Racquet sport      T E N ___ ___ ___

5. Soft and gentle      T E N ___ ___ ___

6. Form of bowling      T E N ___ ___ ___ ___

7. Anxiety or stress      T E N ___ ___ ___ ___

8. Octopus "arm"      T E N ___ ___ ___ ___

*Morning Jumpstarts: Reading, Grade 5* © 2013 Scholastic Teaching Resources

Name _____ Date _____

**WORD of the Day**

Use the word below in a short paragraph about steering a craft in outer space or along the ocean floor.

**navigate:** (v.) *sail, manage, or steer a vessel or vehicle*

_____

_____

_____

## Sentence Mender

**Rewrite the sentence to make it correct.**

She were born in troy new York on January 9 2,012.

_____

## Cursive Quote

**Copy the quotation in cursive writing.**

*If you judge people, you have no time to love them.*

—Mother Teresa of Calcutta

_____

_____

_____

Why do you think this is or is not true? Write your answer in cursive on another sheet of paper.

## Analogy of the Day

**Complete the analogy.**

**Purple** is to **color** as _____ is to **music.**

○ A. jazz     ○ B. red     ○ C. loud     ○ D. fantasy

Explain how the analogy works: _____

_____

## 📖 Ready, Set, READ!

**Read the passage. Then answer the questions.**

Do you like trying different kinds of foods? Do you enjoy writing? If so, you might be interested in what a food writer does. Food writers eat at restaurants and write reviews of the meals. They describe what they like and what they don't. People read the reviews to help them decide whether to visit—or avoid— a restaurant.

Good food critics have to know a lot about ingredients, foods, cooking, and serving. Above all, food critics have to be good writers. They endeavor to describe tastes and textures clearly and in a way that makes readers hungry.

People who read food reviews want to know which dishes the reviewer likes best. They like to learn about a chef's specialties. They want to know what the restaurant looks like or how noisy it is. They want to know whether they have to call ahead to get a table, or whether they can just drop in and start chowing down.

1. What skills does a food writer need to have?

_____

_____

2. What do you think the word *endeavor* means? _____

_____

## ☺ BrainTeaser ☺

Homophones sound the same but have different spellings *and* meanings.

**Write the correct word in each sentence.**

1. We're all here _____ Jackie.  **accept** *or* **except**

2. Only ten students _____ the test.  **passed** *or* **past**

3. Droughts _____ all living things.  **affect** *or* **effect**

4. She _____ at the abstract art.  **stares** *or* **stairs**

5. We can't tell _____ he's awake.  **weather** *or* **whether**

6. May I invite an overnight _____?  **guessed** *or* **guest**

*Morning Jumpstarts: Reading, Grade 5* © 2013 Scholastic Teaching Resources

Name _____  Date _____

Use the word below in a short paragraph about a runner or race.

**spurt**: (v.) *flow out suddenly in a stream or jet; put forth a burst of energy*

_____

_____

_____

## Sentence Mender

**Rewrite the sentence to make it correct.**

Either Jack, Ilsa, and andrew will enter a muffin resippy in the context.

_____

## Cursive Quote

**Copy the quotation in cursive writing.**

*Don't wait for people to be friendly, show them how.*

—Author unknown

**Is this good advice? Explain why. Write your answer in cursive on another sheet of paper.**

## Analogy of the Day

**Complete the analogy.**

**Flame** is to **bright** as _____ is to **waxy**.

○ A. candle    ○ B. water    ○ C. heat    ○ D. lamp

Explain how the analogy works: _____

_____

 # Ready, Set, READ!

**Read the passage. Then answer the questions.**

The kiwi is an unusual bird, about the size of a chicken. It's got a long beak with nostrils and has a round, brown body. The kiwi lays the biggest egg in relation to its size of any bird in the world. And it can't fly. It was named by the Maori people of New Zealand for the memorable sound that it makes.

You may not get the chance to see this rare creature because fewer than 15 zoos outside of New Zealand have them. But you can see a kiwi fruit by visiting any supermarket. Named for the bird because of the way it looks, the kiwi is a rich source of vitamin C and several other vitamins. Go try one. It's delicious!

1. What about the kiwi is true?
   - A. It is a Maori.
   - B. It is named for a fruit.
   - C. There are fewer than 15 left.
   - D. It is flightless.

2. What does a kiwi fruit look like?
   - A. It has a long neck.
   - B. It is as big as a chicken.
   - C. It is round and brown.
   - D. It is big and egg-shaped.

# ⊙ BrainTeaser ⊙

Unscramble each word. Write it correctly in the spaces. Then unscramble the boxed letters to name a math organizer.

_____

ARPEP  ☐ _ _ _ _

HEGIT  _ _ ☐ _ _

AIYLD  _ _ ☐ _ _

HAMSS  _ _ _ _ ☐

TREGE  _ ☐ _ _ _

*Morning Jumpstarts: Reading, Grade 5* © 2013 Scholastic Teaching Resources

Name _____ Date _____

## WORD of the Day

Use the word below in a short paragraph about a person who lives alone or likes to be alone.

**solitary**: (adj.) *alone; away from people; lonely*

_____

_____

_____

## Sentence Mender

Rewrite the sentence to make it correct.

Hay where are you going with my sell phone.

_____

## Cursive Quote

Copy the quotation in cursive writing.

*Time is a circus, always packing up and moving away.*

—Ben Hecht

What else might time be like? Write your answer in cursive on another sheet of paper.

## Analogy of the Day

Complete the analogy.

**Peril** is to **danger** as _____ is to **stream**.

○ A. shore    ○ B. drown    ○ C. ocean    ○ D. brook

Explain how the analogy works: _____

_____

## 📖 Ready, Set, READ!

Read the recipe.
Then answer the questions.

Here is how to make a batch
of 15 delicious pancakes.*
**Prep time: 2 min**
**Cook time: 3 min per batch**

**Ingredients:**
1¼ cups fat-free milk
1 egg
2 cups pancake mix

1. Mix egg and milk together. Pour over pancake mix. Stir until just blended.

2. Pour batter onto hot griddle, ¼ cup at a time.

3. Cook until bubbles break on surface. Turn. Cook until golden.

* For melt-in-your-mouth flavor, add 2 tablespoons of sugar and 1 teaspoon of vanilla into the batter.

**Nutritional information:** 1 serving
(3 pancakes): 200 calories, 4 g fat

1. What do you think *Prep time* is for?

_____

_____

_____

_____

_____

2. What is the purpose of the asterisk (*) following *delicious pancakes*?

_____

_____

_____

_____

_____

3. How many grams of fat are in the

whole batch? _____

## ꩜ BrainTeaser ꩜

A *palindrome* is a word spelled the same backward and forward.
*Mom* and *Otto* are two examples of palindromes.

**Follow the directions below to write your own palindromes.**
• Write four different three-letter palindromes.
• Write three different four-letter palindromes.
• Write two different five-letter palindromes.

_____   _____   _____

_____   _____   _____

_____

54

Name _____ Date _____

## WORD of the Day

Use the word below in a short paragraph about how to change the form of an object or material.

**convert**: (v.) *change something into a different form*

_____

_____

_____

## Sentence Mender

**Rewrite the sentence to make it correct.**

The shef realize that she needs more pepper salt and onion in the Stu.

_____

## Cursive Quote

**Copy the quotation in cursive writing.**

*It is far easier to start something than it is to finish it.*

—Amelia Earhart

What have you started, but not finished? Write your answer in cursive on another sheet of paper.

## Analogy of the Day

**Complete the analogy.**

**Star** is to **constellation** as _____ is to **faculty**.

○ A. planet   ○ B. school   ○ C. teacher   ○ D. student

Explain how the analogy works: _____

_____

# 📖 Ready, Set, READ!

**Read the passage. Then answer the questions.**

Baseball has provided no shortage of memorable moments. Perhaps the greatest of them all took place in Game 1 of the 1988 World Series between the powerful Oakland Athletics and the underdog Los Angeles Dodgers.

The most valuable player on the Dodgers that year was Kirk Gibson, an intense competitor. He was their best hitter and a leader in the clubhouse. But at the end of the season, he injured his leg. He could barely walk. Gibson would not be playing in the World Series. It was a tough blow for the Dodgers and their fans.

Before Game 1, Gibson took batting practice anyway. He grunted in pain with every swing. But he hoped that maybe he could pinch-hit and help his team even a little. He would get his chance in the ninth inning.

The Dodgers were down 4–3 and Oakland's best reliever was pitching. One man was on base. The crowd roared as Gibson hobbled from the dugout to the batter's box.

The count went full. Tension filled the stadium as the pitcher wound up and threw. Gibson grimaced and swung. He connected soundly and the ball sailed over the right field fence. Home run! Game over! Gibson limped around the bases in triumph, pumping his fist and smiling through his pain.

The inspired Dodgers went on to win the Series. Those who witnessed Kirk Gibson's heroics will never forget it.

1. What happened to make the Dodgers even bigger underdogs?

_____

_____

2. What about Gibson's achievement was heroic and memorable?

_____

_____

# ☺ BrainTeaser ☺

Write an antonym from the word bank for each boldface word below.

**Word Bank**

feast   flee   lose   merciful
mild   reject   sensible   sluggish

1. **assume** responsibility _____

2. **severe** weather _____

3. **pursue** the wild game _____

4. **obtain** permission _____

5. **pitiless** judge _____

6. **absurd** excuse _____

7. lengthy **famine** _____

8. at a **brisk** pace _____

56

Name _____ Date _____

## WORD of the Day

Use the word below in a short paragraph about a person or family moving to a place where jobs may be more plentiful.

**migrant**: (n.) *a human who moves from one place to settle in another*

_____

_____

_____

## Sentence Mender

**Rewrite the sentence to make it correct.**

I finely got to play for the maestro, but him was'nt impressed with my effert.

_____

## Cursive Quote

**Copy the quotation in cursive writing.**

*Do what you can, with what you have, where you are.*

—Theodore Roosevelt

What do you think Roosevelt thought about complainers or people who always made excuses? Write your answer in cursive on another sheet of paper.

## Analogy of the Day

**Complete the analogy.**

**Ladder** is to **reach** as _____ is to **cook**.

○ A. restaurant      ○ B. stove      ○ C. fork      ○ D. table

Explain how the analogy works: _____

_____

## 📖 Ready, Set, READ!

Read the advertisement for a new toothpaste.
Then follow the directions.

> *Powerbrush* is the #1 toothpaste! Dentists agree that it works best. All kids say it tastes best. Parents love it. Buy five or more tubes of this whitening wonder now and we will send you a free poster. Look for *Powerbrush* in the best drug stores. Hurry while the supply lasts!

Don't believe everything you read in an advertisement without carefully thinking about it. Write three questions you would like to ask the advertiser to challenge its claims for this toothpaste.

1. _____

_____

2. _____

_____

3. _____

_____

## 🌀 BrainTeaser 🌀

Fill both sides of the antonym box with examples. Write three words in each side. One example is done for you.

| Sweet | Bitter | | Good | Bad |
|-------|--------|---|------|-----|
| sugary | sour | | | |
| | | | | |
| | | | | |

58

*Morning Jumpstarts: Reading, Grade 5* © 2013 Scholastic Teaching Resources

Name _____  Date _____

## WORD of the Day

Use the word below in a short paragraph about something you wish there was more of or less of.

**numerous:** (adj.) *very many*

_____

_____

_____

## Sentence Mender

**Rewrite the sentence to make it correct.**

After triping on a gopher whole in the pastor, she couldn't hardly walk.

_____

## Cursive Quote

**Copy the quotation in cursive writing.**

*Laughter is the shortest distance between two people.*

—Victor Borge

_____

_____

_____

**What do you think Borge meant? Write your answer in cursive on another sheet of paper.**

## Analogy of the Day

**Complete the analogy.**

**Enemy** is to **friend** as _____ is to **tense.**

○ A. present      ○ B. buddy      ○ C. bitter      ○ D. calm

Explain how the analogy works: _____

_____

## 📖 Ready, Set, READ!

**Read the passage. Then answer the questions.**

It had rained heavily for several days. Then, on May 3, 1889, the South Fork Dam failed. It took only 40 minutes for the whole reservoir behind it to empty. Twenty million tons of water was unleashed onto the city of Johnstown, Pennsylvania.

Creeks filled with flowing debris. Trees were ripped out of the ground and telegraph lines got knocked down. Rail lines were washed away. Within a few days, Clara Barton and her new Red Cross arrived to help. Barton stayed on for five months.

The Johnstown Flood was the largest and most shattering natural disaster of the 19th century in America. More than 2,200 people died. Only in the 1900 Galveston hurricane and the 2001 attack on the World Trade Center did more American civilians perish. The flood has been the theme of paintings, stories, and songs. It's been retold in books and in movies. And the story may not be over. Flooding is still a concern for the people of Johnstown today.

1. What happened on May 3, 1889?
   - ○ A. It began to rain.
   - ○ B. The Red Cross arrived.
   - ○ C. There was a hurricane.
   - ○ D. The dam failed.

2. Which is *not* true about the flood?
   - ○ A. It caused great damage.
   - ○ B. It lasted for five months.
   - ○ C. Thousands died.
   - ○ D. The dam emptied in 40 minutes.

## ☺ BrainTeaser ☺

**Use the clues to complete each word that ends in *x*.**

1. Beast of burden          ___ X

2. Combine                  ___ ___ X

3. Highest point            ___ ___ ___ X

4. Cause bad luck           ___ ___ ___ X

5. Encourage with kindness  ___ ___ ___ X

6. Take it easy             ___ ___ ___ ___ X

7. Part of a reference book ___ ___ ___ ___ X

8. Gooey stuff that clogs hearing  ___ ___ ___ ___ ___ X

Name _____ Date _____

## WORD of the Day

Use the word below in a short paragraph about someone putting himself or herself in danger.

**endanger:** (v.) *put someone or something in harm's way*

_____

_____

_____

## Sentence Mender

**Rewrite the sentence to make it correct.**

The singer now have won a oscar and a grammy award.

_____

## Cursive Quote

**Copy the quotation in cursive writing.**

*Ask advice from everyone, but act with your own mind.*

—Yiddish proverb

**Is this good advice? Explain why. Write your answer in cursive on another sheet of paper.**

## Analogy of the Day

**Complete the analogy.**

**Plant** is to **harvest** as _____ is to **drink**.

○ A. tea      ○ B. pour      ○ C. apple      ○ D. glass

Explain how the analogy works: _____

_____

# JUMPSTART 27

## 📖 Ready, Set, READ!

**Read the passage. Then answer the questions.**

They've got magic, kings, evil people, and talking animals. Sometimes they're scary, even violent. They often teach lessons about right and wrong. Some warn children of the dangers in the world. They are fairy tales. Two hundred years ago, two German brothers became fascinated by them.

Jacob and William Grimm were born a year apart. They were very close and shared many interests. They lived together. They studied and taught together. And they decided to begin collecting fairy tales and writing them down. Soon they published their first of many books of this genre. The world has been enchanted by them ever since.

Cinderella, Snow White, Rapunzel, and Hansel and Gretel were characters in the more than 200 tales the brothers Grimm gathered and published. They included many illustrations in their books, too. And as they came upon new tales, they added them. *Grimm's Fairy Tales* are read and loved by children around the world.

1. What makes fairy tales important?

_____

_____

_____

_____

_____

_____

2. What do you think the word *genre* means?

_____

_____

_____

_____

_____

_____

## ๑ BrainTeaser ๑

Write *a*, *e*, *i*, *o*, or *u* to finish spelling each baseball word.

1. b ____ llp ____ n

2. sh ____ rtst ____ p

3. d ____ ____ bl ____

4. ____ mp ____ r ____

5. d ____ g ____ ____ t

6. b ____ ckst ____ p

7. i ____ f ____ ____ ld

8. bl ____ ____ ch ____ rs

9. m ____ n ____ g ____ r

10. r ____ ____ k ____ ____

Morning Jumpstarts: Reading, Grade 5 © 2013 Scholastic Teaching Resources

Name _____ Date _____

## WORD of the Day

Use the word below in a short paragraph about things you and your friends have in common.

**peer:** (n.) *someone who has the same rank, ability, or qualities as another person; equal*

_____

_____

_____

## Sentence Mender

**Rewrite the sentence to make it correct.**

Both her and nina mist the sience test.

_____

## Cursive Quote

**Copy the quotation in cursive writing.**

*Whatever creativity is, it is in part a solution to a problem.*

—Brian Aldiss

_____

_____

_____

How have you solved a problem creatively? Write your answer in cursive on another sheet of paper.

## Analogy of the Day

**Complete the analogy.**

**Train** is to **track** as _____ is to **sea**.

○ A. caboose     ○ B. diver     ○ C. ship     ○ D. beach

Explain how the analogy works: _____

_____

**Ready, Set, READ!**

Read the Cherokee legend that explains the origin of diseases and medicine. Then answer the questions.

Humans and animals once lived together in harmony. But as the human population grew, people had to kill more animals for their meat, feathers, and skins. The animals were upset. They decided to do something about it. The deer acted first. Their elders decided that if a hunter killed a deer and did not ask forgiveness, a fast deer would go find the hunter and strike him with a punishing disease.

Like the deer, other animals, even insects, came up with ways to punish humans who hunted them. The animals were fighting back. They even invented new illnesses to use. Lucky for humans, plants came to their rescue. They did not wish to see all humans wiped out. So, they held a meeting. The plants decided that each one would be a source of medicine for one of the diseases the animals caused. It was up to the humans to figure out which plant cured which disease.

1. What do you think *live in harmony* means? _____

_____

2. Who came to the humans' rescue? What did they do?

_____

_____

## BrainTeaser

**What do you call a person who always wires for money?**

Solve each clue. Then copy each letter into its numbered box to find the answer to the riddle.

• Water from the sky  __ __ __ __
                       8  12  9  13

• Make a knot  __ __ __
               7  11  5

• End a subscription  __ __ __ __ __ __
                      10  1  2  6  3  4

| 1 | 2 | | 3 | 4 | 5 | 6 | 7 | 8 | 9 | 10 | 11 | 12 | 13 |
|---|---|---|---|---|---|---|---|---|---|----|----|----|----|
|   |   | |   |   |   |   |   |   |   |    |    |    |    |

*Morning Jumpstarts: Reading, Grade 5 © 2013 Scholastic Teaching Resources*

Name _____ Date _____

## WORD of the Day

Use the word below in a short paragraph about almost doing something foolish.

**senseless:** (adj.) *foolish; stupid*

_____

_____

_____

## Sentence Mender

**Rewrite the sentence to make it correct.**

Miguel told victor that he didnt need to practiss no more.

_____

## Cursive Quote

**Copy the quotation in cursive writing.**

*A bit of fragrance always clings to the hand that gives roses.*

—Chinese proverb

_____

_____

_____

What do you think this proverb means? Write your answer in cursive on another sheet of paper.

## Analogy of the Day

**Complete the analogy.**

**Screen** is to **television** as _____ is to **school**.

○ A. classroom      ○ B. work      ○ C. bus      ○ D. neighborhood

Explain how the analogy works: _____

_____

# Ready, Set, READ!

**Read the passage. Then answer the questions.**

The Hudson is more than a river.

In 1609, Dutch explorer Henry Hudson sailed the *Half Moon* into what is now the New York harbor. As he sailed north up the passage, he did not discover a water route west to Asia as he thought he might have. But he did discover a river that now bears his name.

A *river* is a large natural stream of water that empties into an ocean or lake. Hudson sailed up his river far enough to see that for himself. But the Hudson is something else, too. It is an estuary. An *estuary* is the mouth of a river, where the flowing sea tide meets the river's current. Where the Hudson passes the island of Manhattan, it is an estuary. And the Hudson is more than a river and an estuary. It is also a fjord. A *fjord* is an inlet that is long and narrow and bordered by high cliffs. It is formed by a glacier.

Henry Hudson discovered more than he knew.

1. A narrow passage of water bordered by cliffs is called a(n)
   - ○ A. island.
   - ○ B. half moon.
   - ○ C. fjord.
   - ○ D. estuary.

2. Where is an estuary?
   - ○ A. on the moon
   - ○ B. in every fjord
   - ○ C. in any passage
   - ○ D. at the mouth of a river

3. What did Henry Hudson hope to discover?
   - ○ A. a glacier
   - ○ B. the moon
   - ○ C. a waterway to Asia
   - ○ D. the island of Manhattan

# ⊚ BrainTeaser ⊚

**Think of one word that all three words on the left have in common. Write it on the line. The first one is done for you.**

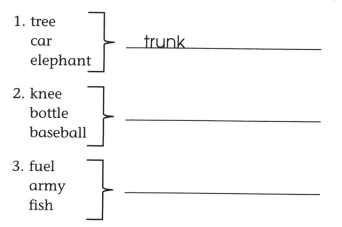

1. tree
   car
   elephant — trunk

2. knee
   bottle
   baseball — _____

3. fuel
   army
   fish — _____

4. license
   home
   paper — _____

5. baby
   olive
   motor — _____

6. string
   cottage
   cheddar — _____

**66**

*Morning Jumpstarts: Reading, Grade 5* © 2013 Scholastic Teaching Resources

Name _____ Date _____

## WORD of the Day

Use the word below in a short paragraph about something you would like your friends to write down and remember.

**dictate**: (v.) *say or read something aloud for another person to write down or a machine to record*

_____

_____

_____

## Sentence Mender

**Rewrite the sentence to make it correct.**

then he poured the cereal and first he addeded fruit and milk.

_____

## Cursive Quote

**Copy the quotation in cursive writing.**

*Tomorrow belongs to the people who prepare for it today.*

—African proverb

_____

_____

_____

**Do you agree? Explain. Write your answer in cursive on another sheet of paper.**

## Analogy of the Day

**Complete the analogy.**

**Violin** is to **musician** as _____ is to **golfer**.

○ A. guitar    ○ B. swing    ○ C. course    ○ D. club

Explain how the analogy works: _____

_____

# Side B

## 📖 Ready, Set, READ!

**Read the passage. Then answer the questions.**

Before there were photographs, people didn't know what the American West looked like. It took the work of artists to show them. One of these painters was Albert Bierstadt (1830–1902). His work showed the grandeur of the western mountains, rivers, and waterfalls. His huge canvases were beautiful. They were inspiring. They demanded attention.

The German-born painter was a member of a group of like-minded artists known as the Hudson River School. These painters interpreted American vistas in heroic ways.

Like others who painted western scenes, Bierstadt took several trips there to better know his subject. He altered the features of what he painted with bold, exaggerated colors. He made full use of sunlight, clouds, mist, rainbows, and fog. His lush landscapes can take your breath away. They are better liked now than when he painted them. Go to see his work. It is on display in art museums across the country. You can also see some of his paintings online.

1. What did the painters of the Hudson River School have in common?

_____

_____

2. What does the expression *take your breath away* mean?

_____

_____

3. Where can you see Bierstadt's work if you can't visit a museum?

_____

## 🌀 BrainTeaser 🌀

**Each sentence below has two blanks. Both use the same letters to form two different words. Fill them in.**

1. Is she _____ to move that _____ of hay?

2. _____ on the hot soup in your _____ to cool it off.

3. Which _____ do we need to fix the broken _____?

4. Let's _____ off the muddy porch after the sun has _____.

5. I can't believe those _____ _____ for such a silly photo!

68

*Morning Jumpstarts: Reading, Grade 5 © 2013 Scholastic Teaching Resources*

Name _____   Date _____

## WORD of the Day

Use the word below in a short paragraph about an accomplishment.

**achievement:** (n.) *something accomplished by hard work*

_____

_____

_____

## Sentence Mender

**Rewrite the sentence to make it correct.**

Many peoples get sick from mosquitoe bytes.

_____

## Cursive Quote

**Copy the quotation in cursive writing.**

*The bamboo that bends is stronger than the oak that persists.*

—Japanese proverb

_____

_____

_____

**What do you think this proverb means? Write your answer in cursive on another sheet of paper.**

## Analogy of the Day

**Complete the analogy.**

**Exercise** is to **sweating** as _____ is to **weeping**.

○ A. celebrate     ○ B. tears     ○ C. sadness     ○ D. crying

Explain how the analogy works: _____

_____

## 📖 Ready, Set, READ!

**Read the passage. Then answer the questions.**

In the 1700s, a group of Muscogee Indians moved south into the grassy plains of northern Florida. They were called Creeks because they placed their villages near creeks. They moved to get away from warring tribes in Georgia.

Other Native American groups soon joined the Creeks. So did free blacks and runaway slaves. Together they formed the Seminoles. To some colonists the name meant "runaway." To others, it meant "wild," like a bear is wild.

In 1818, the U.S. Army attacked the Seminoles. They did so to capture slaves hiding with the tribe. The Seminoles fought back, and then retreated south into the Everglades. The army attacked again in the 1830s. Many members of the tribe were forced to leave. They were resettled onto reservations far away. But some stayed deep in the swamps, undefeated and proud. There they have remained.

These American citizens now have modern jobs and live modern lives. But they have kept their old ways alive. They speak English and also a Muscogee language. And some still participate in the ancient rites of their ancestors.

1. Why did the Creeks leave Georgia? _____

_____

2. Why do you think some saw the Seminoles as wild?

_____

_____

## ꙮ BrainTeaser ꙮ

**Pick an interesting person, place, or thing. Name it on the first line below. Write 26 adjectives to describe your choice. Begin each word with a different letter, using every letter from *a* to *z*.**

_____ is . . . _____

_____

_____

_____

*Morning Jumpstarts: Reading, Grade 5* © 2013 Scholastic Teaching Resources

Name _____ Date _____

## WORD of the Day

Use the word below in a short paragraph about what a region, place, or building looks like.

**visual:** (adj.) *having to do with sight*

_____

_____

_____

## Sentence Mender

Rewrite the sentence to make it correct.

Before labor day, we was happy and everything seamed perfict.

_____

## Cursive Quote

Copy the quotation in cursive writing.

*The good we do today becomes the happiness of tomorrow.*

—William James

_____

_____

_____

Was James correct? Explain. Write your answer in cursive on another sheet of paper.

## Analogy of the Day

Complete the analogy.

**Terrier** is to **dog** as _____ is to **flower**.

○ A. cat      ○ B. rose      ○ C. tree      ○ D. plant

Explain how the analogy works: _____

_____

## 📖 Ready, Set, READ!

**Read the passage. Then answer the questions.**

Songwriting is a career some musical people pursue. Some write popular tunes. Others may write funny songs, religious songs, or songs for musical theater. Some write songs for individuals to sing. Others write them for large choruses.

There were no full-time professional songwriters in America in Stephen Foster's time. That was until he gave it a go. Foster wrote songs many people still sing today. There are his sweet ballads, like "My Old Kentucky Home" and "Beautiful Dreamer." There are his knee-slapping tunes, like "Nelly Bly" and "Camptown Races." But writing songs was not an easy way to make a living in 1850. Foster's beloved "Oh! Susanna" earned him a mere $100.

Stephen Foster wrote hundreds of songs. But he died in poverty. He was only 37 years old. Happily, in our time the "father of American music" has gotten the recognition denied him in his own day. Forty years ago he was inducted into the Songwriters Hall of Fame. In 2010, the Nashville Songwriters Hall of Fame did him the same honor. Which of his songs can you sing?

1. What was unusual about the career Foster chose?

_____

_____

2. What impression about life as an artist does this passage give?

_____

_____

## ⊚ BrainTeaser ⊚

Imagine a long journey to any place in the world. Write 26 verbs for actions, conditions, or experiences you might have along the way. Begin each word with a different letter, using every letter from *a* to *z*.

On my journey to _____ , I will _____

_____

_____

*Morning Jumpstarts: Reading, Grade 5* © 2013 Scholastic Teaching Resources

Name _____ Date _____

## WORD of the Day

Use the word below in a short paragraph explaining why you should be allowed to do something your parents won't let you do.

**justify:** (v.) *give a good reason for something; show that something is right or just*

_____

_____

_____

## Sentence Mender

**Rewrite the sentence to make it correct.**

"There is bear tracks ahead on the trail, so be carful, the ranger warn."

_____

## Cursive Quote

**Copy the quotation in cursive writing.**

*You have to expect things of yourself before you can do them.*

—Michael Jordan

_____

_____

_____

**Do you think this is true for everyone? Explain. Write your answer in cursive on another sheet of paper.**

## Analogy of the Day

**Complete the analogy.**

**Annoy** is to **please** as _____ is to **hate**.

○ A. love     ○ B. pester     ○ C. thank     ○ D. spinach

Explain how the analogy works: _____

_____

## Ready, Set, READ!

**Read the e-mail. Then answer the questions.**

From: Katie
Date: 9/17/1903
To: Lamar
Subject: wow!!!

Hi Lamar!
I know e-mail hasn't been invented yet, but I simply had to hurry up and write so I could tell someone what I've just seen. OMG. You'd better sit down. You are not going to believe this.

So, Lamar, I'm here at something-Hawk on the Outer Banks, walking with my aunt's dogs. (She's got a place here.) I'm looking over at this field and what do I see coming my way? With my own two eyes I watch this flimsy-looking thing with wings. And it's got a guy lying down on it wearing goggles. Then, guess what? This machine lifts off the ground and glides through the air right at me! Right at me! I dropped to the ground and covered my head. The dogs went nuts as it flew right over us. UNBELIEVABLE! You know that pond in back of the Jones place? That thing flew far enough to go over it. You won't see something like this every day. Tell Curtis! Tell Wilbur! Tell everybody! :)

See ya, Katie

1. What did Katie witness?

_____
_____
_____
_____
_____
_____
_____

2. What about this story makes it a fantasy?

_____
_____
_____
_____
_____
_____
_____

## ⑨ BrainTeaser ⑥

The sentence in the box has only seven words.
But every word starts with the *same* letter.

**Write a sentence in which every word begins with _t_.**
**Make it as long as you can.**

> **D**octor **D**ouglas **d**elays **d**ifficult **d**ecisions **d**uring **d**aylight.

_____
_____

Name _____ Date _____

## WORD of the Day

Use the word below in a short paragraph describing how the country would be different if you were in charge.

**reign**: (n.) *the period or power of a ruler*

_____

_____

_____

## Sentence Mender

**Rewrite the sentence to make it correct.**

Henry wondered whom winned the world series last year?

_____

## Cursive Quote

**Copy the quotation in cursive writing.**

*Lack of patience in small matters can create havoc in great ones.*

—Chinese proverb

**What do you think this proverb means? Write your answer in cursive on another sheet of paper.**

## Analogy of the Day

**Complete the analogy.**

**Bright** is to **brilliant** as _____ is to **exhilarated**.

○ A. miserable     ○ B. delighted     ○ C. calm     ○ D. careful

Explain how the analogy works: _____

_____

# 📖 Ready, Set, READ!

**Read the passage. Then answer the questions.**

In 1930, Percival Lowell was looking through his telescope in Arizona. He found a distant object orbiting the sun. That object became the ninth planet in our solar system. It was given the name Pluto. Pluto was the Roman god of the underworld. Perhaps the object got the name because it was so far away from the sun and orbited in darkness.

Pluto is much smaller than the other planets. In fact, it is smaller than our moon. Scientists have since discovered several other objects like it in the outer solar system. They have changed the meaning of what a planet is because of those discoveries. Pluto's life as a planet came to an end. There are now only eight planets in our solar system.

Lowell's find is now called a "dwarf planet." A spacecraft heading toward Pluto left earth in 2006. It is expected to reach it in 2015. Then we may learn much more about this dwarf planet and its four tiny moons.

1. Why did Lowell think he had discovered a new planet?
   - ○ A. He loved Roman myths.
   - ○ B. It orbited the sun.
   - ○ C. It had been hard to find.
   - ○ D. It was so far away.

2. Why is Pluto no longer called a planet?
   - ○ A. It does not orbit the sun.
   - ○ B. It has only four moons.
   - ○ C. It is too small.
   - ○ D. It is too far from the sun.

3. Which is *not* true about Pluto?
   - ○ A. It has four moons.
   - ○ B. It was named after a Roman god.
   - ○ C. It is smaller than our moon.
   - ○ D. It was discovered in 2006.

# ☺ BrainTeaser ☺

Climb the word ladder to change *hush* to *yell*. Change only one letter at a time. Write the new word on each step.

yell

hush

Name _____ Date _____

## WORD of the Day

Use the word below in a short paragraph about a time you did not get the reaction you wanted or expected.

**negative:** (adj.) *saying no; not positive*

_____

_____

_____

## Sentence Mender

Rewrite the sentence to make it correct.

I red an article called how to joining social Networks.

_____

## Cursive Quote

Copy the quotation in cursive writing.

*If you see no reason for giving thanks, the fault lies in yourself.*

—Native American proverb, Minquass tribe

Do you agree? Explain. Write your answer in cursive on another sheet of paper.

## Analogy of the Day

Complete the analogy.

**See** is to **view** as _____ is to **sleep.**

○ A. awaken     ○ B. snooze     ○ C. tired     ○ D. snore

Explain how the analogy works: _____

_____

# 📖 Ready, Set, READ!

Read the poem. Then answer the questions.

### The Dog
*by Ogden Nash*

The truth I do not stretch or shove
When I state the dog is full of love.
I've also found, by actual test,
A wet dog is the lovingest.

1. What does it mean to *not stretch or shove* the truth?

_____

_____

2. Do you think the poet gave the dog a "love test"? Explain.

_____

_____

3. What does the poet *really* mean in the last line?

_____

_____

# ⊚ BrainTeaser ⊚

What does each saying mean? Read the definitions on the right.
Write the number on the line.

1. Let's **turn over a new leaf**.

2. Don't be a **backseat driver**.

3. She's finally **off the hook**.

4. Will you **make the grade**?

5. They are **on pins and needles**.

6. They try to **make ends meet**.

7. The couch cost **an arm and a leg**.

_____ qualify

_____ waiting nervously

_____ no longer needed

_____ was very expensive

_____ pay all their expenses

_____ make a change for the better

_____ one who offers unwanted advice

*Morning Jumpstarts: Reading, Grade 5* © 2013 Scholastic Teaching Resources

Name _____ Date _____

## WORD of the Day

Use the word below in a short paragraph about something subtle that you spotted, sniffed, felt, heard, or tasted.

**detect:** (v.) *discover something that is hard to notice*

_____

_____

_____

## Sentence Mender

**Rewrite the sentence to make it correct.**

The umpire state Building is more taller then the Chrysler building.

_____

## Cursive Quote

**Copy the quotation in cursive writing.**

*If you don't have confidence, you'll always find a way not to win.*

—Carl Lewis

Rewrite Lewis's quote without using the negative words. Do you agree with the new statement? Write your explanation in cursive on another sheet of paper.

## Analogy of the Day

**Complete the analogy.**

**Employee** is to **company** as _____ is to **mammal**.

○ A. zoo     ○ B. fur     ○ C. whale     ○ D. reptile

Explain how the analogy works: _____

_____

 # Ready, Set, READ!

**Read the letter. Then answer the questions.**

Dear Mr. and Mrs. Lopez,

I wish to be considered for the position of dog walker that you have advertised. I am 12 years old and very grown up for my age. My family has a chocolate lab that I care for. And I already walk a golden retriever and a boxer. So you see that I am comfortable handling large dogs.

I am available for walks before and after school each day. I can walk your dog on the weekends, too. Also, I could watch Gracie if you go away. We have an extra doggie bed here, and Nellie likes to have guests.

I can provide references. And I can start right away.

I look forward to hearing from you. You can reach me at 555-0115.

Sincerely,
Michelle K.

1. What is true about Gracie?
   - ○ A. She is large.
   - ○ B. She is friendly.
   - ○ C. She is a golden color.
   - ○ D. She is Michelle's dog.

2. What fact did Michelle leave out in her letter?
   - ○ A. her availability
   - ○ B. her fee
   - ○ C. her qualifications
   - ○ D. her age

3. What do you think is Michelle's best qualification?

   _____

   _____

   _____

   _____

   _____

# BrainTeaser

**What lies in a junkyard and twitches?**

Solve each clue. Then copy each letter into its numbered box to find the answer to the riddle.

- Blinker on a computer screen  ___ ___ ___ ___ ___ ___
  12  7  10  8  6  4

- Vehicle used for moving  ___ ___ ___
  5  1  2

- Seven days  ___ ___ ___ ___
  9  11  3  13

| 1 | | 2 | 3 | 4 | 5 | 6 | 7 | 8 | | 9 | 10 | 11 | 12 | 13 |
|---|---|---|---|---|---|---|---|---|---|---|----|----|----|----|

**80**

Name _____ Date _____

## WORD of the Day

Use the word below in a short paragraph about a time something or somebody got in the way.

**obstacle:** (n.) *something that gets in the way*

_____

_____

_____

## Sentence Mender

Rewrite the sentence to make it correct.

Matt clark opened the door and steps out.

_____

## Cursive Quote

Copy the quotation in cursive writing.

*Life is like a ten-speed bike. Most of us have gears we never use.*

—Charles Schultz

_____

_____

_____

Have you used all your gears? Explain. Write your answer in cursive on another sheet of paper.

## Analogy of the Day

Complete the analogy.

**Hour** is to **day** as _____ is to **bed**.

○ A. breakfast ○ B. night ○ C. sleep ○ D. mattress

Explain how the analogy works: _____

_____

## 📖 Ready, Set, READ!

**Read the passage. Then answer the questions.**

*Monster on Campus*, a movie review

Do you want to be terrified? Do you want nightmares for weeks about a vicious giant sea creature? If you do, then *do not* waste your money on *Monster on Campus*. Avoid this silly movie like you would an annoying little cousin!

But if what you want is to giggle at a monster so unscary that you want to take it home and cuddle it, this movie is for you. And if you want characters so unlikeable that you want them to be eaten as soon as possible, then don't wait another monster moment. Race to the box office.

The movie is set on the campus of a coastal New England boarding school. The teachers have guppy faces. The bricks on the buildings look like scales. The grounds are soggy and puddle-filled. The place is creepy enough without a monster. I say, invite the beast in. Dress it in a school uniform and give it a seat in a classroom. Then you'll at least have a documentary about what it's like to be a monster in a new school.

1. What does the reviewer think about this movie?

   _____

   _____

2. How would you describe the tone of the review? Provide support from the passage

   for your view. _____

   _____

   _____

## 🌀 BrainTeaser 🌀

How many different words can you spell with letters from the word *explanation*? Every word must have at least three letters. List them here.

_____

_____

_____

*Morning Jumpstarts: Reading, Grade 5* © 2013 Scholastic Teaching Resources

Name _____ Date _____

## WORD of the Day

Use the word below in a short paragraph about two things that are alike.

**identical**: (adj.) *exactly alike*

_____

_____

_____

## Sentence Mender

**Rewrite the sentence to make it correct.**

The night show his bravery in battel and was rewarded with land and a Title.

_____

## Cursive Quote

**Copy the quotation in cursive writing.**

*What is told in the ear of one person is often heard 100 miles away.*

—Chinese proverb

------------------------------------------------

------------------------------------------------

------------------------------------------------

**What do you think this proverb means? Write your answer in cursive on another sheet of paper.**

## Analogy of the Day

**Complete the analogy.**

**Silk** is to **soft** as _____ is to **rough**.

○ A. clothing    ○ B. flannel    ○ C. sandpaper    ○ D. coarse

Explain how the analogy works: _____

_____

## 📖 Ready, Set, READ!

**Read the passage. Then answer the questions.**

The terrible Civil War was raging. Johnny Clem ran away from home to join the Army. An Ohio regiment wouldn't take him. Nor would one from Michigan. But he tagged along with the Michigan men anyway. He became one of their drummers. His officers made sure he got paid. Johnny was only nine years old.

He got the name "Johnny Shiloh" when a Rebel shell smashed his drum during that great battle. He soon was allowed to trade his drum for a musket. Johnny liked this better. "I did not like to stand and be shot at without shooting back," he said.

Johnny was active in the Army. He carried dispatches for generals. He had a pony shot out from under him. He was wounded twice. After the war he tried to get into West Point, but was rejected for his poor schooling. Still, President Grant appointed him a second lieutenant. Johnny Clem retired from the Army in 1916. His rank: major general.

1. How did Johnny Clem get his start in the Army?

_____

_____

2. What made Johnny an unusual soldier? _____

_____

## ෧ BrainTeaser ෧

Solve the puzzle. It has a two-letter word on top and an eight-letter word at the bottom. Going down, each word uses the same letters as the word above it, plus one more, and then rearranged.

**Clues:**

• nickname for Edward

• lipstick color

• mother of a fawn

• discourage; hinder

• paid the landlord

• adjusted the guitar strings again

• set of false teeth

*Morning Jumpstarts: Reading, Grade 5* © 2013 Scholastic Teaching Resources

Name _____ Date _____

Use the word below in a short paragraph about a book or a movie in which a character is treated cruelly.

**abuse:** (n.) *cruel or rough treatment*

_____

_____

_____

## Sentence Mender

**Rewrite the sentence to make it correct.**

"Were gone to the zoo when the new monkies arrive," said Maxs sister."

_____

## Cursive Quote

**Copy the quotation in cursive writing.**

*Early to bed and early to rise, makes a man healthy, wealthy, and wise.*

—Benjamin Franklin

_____

_____

What do you think about Franklin's advice? Write your answer in cursive on another sheet of paper.

## Analogy of the Day

**Complete the analogy.**

**Easy** is to **challenging** as _____ is to **tricky**.

○ A. puzzle   ○ B. hard   ○ C. confusing   ○ D. simple

Explain how the analogy works: _____

_____

## 📖 Ready, Set, READ!

Read these lyrics from a song Stephen Foster wrote in 1862. Then answer the questions.

**That's What's the Matter!**

We live in hard and stirring times,
Too sad for mirth, too rough for rhymes;
For songs of peace have lost their chimes,
    And that's what's the matter!

The men we held as brothers true,
Have turn'd into a rebel crew;
So now we have to put them thro',
    And that's what's the matter!

Chorus: That's what's the matter,
        The rebels have to scatter;
        We'll make them flee,
        By land and sea,
        And that's what's the matter!

1. What is the matter?

_____

_____

_____

_____

2. On which side of the conflict is the songwriter? How do you know?

_____

_____

_____

_____

3. What does *songs of peace have lost their chimes* mean?

_____

_____

_____

_____

## 🌀 BrainTeaser 🌀

The word bank contains music words. Each word is hidden in the puzzle. Find and circle each word.

| Word Bank | |
|---|---|
| ALTO | LYRICS |
| BAR | NOTES |
| BARITONE | OCTAVE |
| BASS | REST |
| BEAT | RHYTHM |
| CHORD | SHARP |
| CLEF | SOPRANO |
| FLAT | TEMPO |
| HARMONY | TENOR |
| KEY | TUNE |

```
S O A P T B A R I T O N E
O C R E E E L H B U G O T
P L T N N A T Y A N K T L
R E S T O T O T R E K E Y
A F L F R Y C H O R D S R
N U C L H A R M O N Y N I
O C T A V E W S H A R P C
D R E T E M P O K B A S S
```

*Morning Jumpstarts: Reading, Grade 5* © 2013 Scholastic Teaching Resources

Name _____ Date _____

## WORD of the Day

Use the word below in a short paragraph about a time a cool drink really hit the spot.

**beverage:** (n.) *a liquid used or made for drinking*

_____

_____

_____

## Sentence Mender

Rewrite the sentence to make it correct.

It use to be that few College graduates lived with there parent's.

_____

## Cursive Quote

Copy the quotation in cursive writing.

*Kindness is the language which the deaf can hear and the blind can see.*

—Mark Twain

_____

_____

_____

Do you agree with Twain's idea about a common language? Write your answer in cursive on another sheet of paper.

## Analogy of the Day

Complete the analogy.

**Shovel** is to **dig** as _____ is to **music**.

○ A. guitar    ○ B. sweater    ○ C. thread    ○ D. fabric

Explain how the analogy works: _____

_____

 # Ready, Set, READ!

**Read the passage. Then answer the questions.**

Have you ever enjoyed a Chinese egg roll or a Thai spring roll? How about a tasty Mexican burrito or flauta? What about a savory or jam-filled French crêpe or a Russian blini? Have you ever had a delicious Italian cannoli for dessert? If you have eaten any of these, then you've sampled a kind of food that cultures around the world offer. All are varieties of filled breads or pastries that are either baked or fried.

Cannoli

And you don't want to leave the delicious blintz off this list. The blintz arrived in America with European immigrants. It is a thin fried pancake filled with farmer cheese, potato, or fruit. You usually eat a blintz with butter, apple sauce, berries, sour cream, or maybe a dusting of powdered sugar. A blintz makes a wonderful special occasion breakfast treat. It is so good that you won't want to wait for the next special occasion to devour one. You'll find blintzes served at many delis, restaurants, and diners. Or, you can visit your local supermarket. There you'll find them in the frozen foods section—beside the frozen burritos and egg rolls.

Blintz

1. What do all these foods have in common? _____

_____

2. In what ways do they differ?_____

_____

# ☺ BrainTeaser ☺

Each word below has two pairs of double letters that are missing. All missing pairs appear in the letter bank. Fill in some words with two *different* pairs, and others with two of the *same* pair.

1. hi ☐☐ bi ☐☐ y

2. f ☐☐ tba ☐☐

3. a ☐☐ re ☐☐

4. sw ☐☐ tne ☐☐

5. go ☐☐ e ☐☐

6. co ☐☐☐

7. ra ☐☐☐ n

8. dum ☐☐ e ☐☐

**Letter Bank**

BB  CC  DD

EE  FF

LL  OO  SS

Morning Jumpstarts: Reading, Grade 5 © 2013 Scholastic Teaching Resources

# JUMPSTART 41

Name _____ Date _____

## WORD of the Day

Use the word below in a short paragraph about a hot and steamy summer morning.

**hazy:** (adj.) *misty; smoky; dim*

_____

_____

_____

## Sentence Mender

**Rewrite the sentence to make it correct.**

Ethan Ellis and eli is the best tenners in the church quire.

_____

## Cursive Quote

**Copy the quotation in cursive writing.**

*Reading gives us someplace to go when we have to stay where we are.*

—Mason Cooley

_____

_____

_____

What did Cooley mean by *someplace to go*? Write your answer in cursive on another sheet of paper.

## Analogy of the Day

**Complete the analogy.**

**Wrench** is to **mechanic** as _____ is to **painter**.

○ A. painting    ○ B. brush    ○ C. museum    ○ D. gallery

Explain how the analogy works: _____

_____

*Morning Jumpstarts: Reading, Grade 5 © 2013 Scholastic Teaching Resources*

## 📖 Ready, Set, READ!

**Read the passage. Then answer the questions.**

The stories of Icarus or Athena are myths. The story of the tortoise and the hare is a fable.

Myths are stories that explain how the world works or how we should treat one another. They are set in the distant past and feature gods, goddesses, and super-beings that have adventures and make things happen. The word *myth* comes from the Greek word *mythos*, which means "word of mouth." Myths are shared by groups of people and become part of their culture as they are passed along from generation to generation. Similar stories are told by different cultures. For example, most have their versions of how the world came to be.

Fables are stories told to teach a lesson about something. They are like myths in that they have been passed on orally from one generation to the next. Fables are frequently shorter than myths. They also differ in that they make use of talking animals and plants, and even rocks that can move. Like myths, fables were eventually written down.

1. How are myths and fables alike? _____

_____

2. In what ways do they differ?_____

_____

3. Which do you prefer? Explain why. _____

_____

## ๑ BrainTeaser ๑

**Read the clues to solve these puzzling riddles.**

| Clue | What am I? |
|------|------------|
| 1. The more I dry, the wetter I get. | |
| 2. Though I am very heavy, backwards I am not. | |
| 3. You can hear and feel me, but you can never see me. | |
| 4. Put this in a heavy bag of sand to make it lighter. | |
| 5. I run but cannot walk. My mouth can never eat. My bed is not for sleeping. | |

Name _____ Date _____

### WORD of the Day

Use the word below in a short paragraph about a time when you believed something true that turned out not to be.

**assume:** (v.) *take for granted without proof*

_____

_____

_____

## Sentence Mender

**Rewrite the sentence to make it correct.**

Marie curie was a scientist whom was a head of her time.

_____

## Cursive Quote

**Copy the quotation in cursive writing.**

*Every day do something that will inch you closer to a better tomorrow.*

—Doug Firebaugh

_____

_____

_____

**Do you agree? Explain. Write your answer in cursive on another sheet of paper.**

## Analogy of the Day

**Complete the analogy.**

**Desk** is to **office** as _____ is to **ocean.**

○ A. bird     ○ B. sky     ○ C. submarine     ○ D. land

Explain how the analogy works: _____

_____

## 📖 Ready, Set, READ!

**Read the passage. Then answer the questions.**

On the night of October 30, 1938, people listening to a popular radio program got the shock of their lives. They leaned close to their radios to hear the incredible news that Martians had landed on Earth and were attacking. People panicked. Many fled from their homes in terror.

It was all a Halloween hoax. It was the work of actor and director Orson Welles. In the one-hour broadcast of his Mercury Theater on the Air, Welles reported a series of frightening news bulletins. They sounded very real. There were no commercial breaks. That made them sound even more real. Welles based his program on the H. G. Wells novel *The War of the Worlds*. But he updated the alien invasion. It moved from 19th-century England to a small town in New Jersey.

Not everybody was amused. Many protested the wild prank. But that radio episode made Welles a household name. He went on to become a famous movie director.

1. What prank did Welles play? _____

_____

2. How do you think people would react to a radio program like that today?

_____

_____

2. Which is *not* a synonym for *hoax*?
   ○ A. trick    ○ B. swindle    ○ C. prank    ○ D. invasion

## ☺ BrainTeaser ☺

**Use logic to match each person with a job and a score. Use the grid to keep track of what you figure out.**

- Ava, Jorge, and Rex took a test after work one day. Jorge got more right answers than the baker. But he got fewer right answers than Ava did.

- The clerk didn't get as many right answers as the dentist did.

| Person's Name | Person's Job | Score (high, middle, low) |
|---|---|---|
| Ava | | |
| Jorge | | |
| Rex | | |

*Morning Jumpstarts: Reading, Grade 5 © 2013 Scholastic Teaching Resources*

Name _____  Date _____

## WORD of the Day

Use the word below in a short paragraph about why there are food shortages in parts of the world.

**famine:** (n.) *a time of severe food shortage in a region or among a group of people*

_____

_____

_____

## Sentence Mender

Rewrite the sentence to make it correct.

You and me should recieve awards for spelling and grammer grateness.

_____

## Cursive Quote

Copy the quotation in cursive writing.

*If you can, help others; if you cannot do that, at least do not harm them.*

—Randy Rind

Do you agree that it's enough just not to do harm? Write your answer in cursive on another sheet of paper.

## Analogy of the Day

Complete the analogy.

**Knife** is to **cut** as _____ is to **light**.

○ A. glass   ○ B. lamp   ○ C. darkness   ○ D. heavy

Explain how the analogy works: _____

_____

 # Ready, Set, READ!

**Read the passage. Then answer the questions.**

America boasts many national parks. Yellowstone is the oldest and the first in the world. Visitors have been enjoying its wildlife, lakes, geysers, and canyons for more than 140 years. Grand Canyon is probably the most famous of our parks. You can view the amazing canyon from trails along its rim. Or you can hike deep into it to fully appreciate how awesome it is. In addition, you can raft through it on the Colorado River. Our most popular park is Great Smoky Mountains. Millions hike its misty mountains and lush forests each year.

Our most unusual park may be Mammoth Caves. It's different than the others because it's all underground! Visitors to the park can walk miles of underground trails. They can linger in giant rooms with high ceilings, or squeeze through dark and narrow tunnels. They can marvel at jaw-dropping rock formations 300 feet below the ground. Mammoth Caves is in Kentucky, just north of Nashville, Tennessee.

1. Which park gets the most visitors?
   - ○ A. Grand Canyon
   - ○ B. Yellowstone
   - ○ C. Mammoth Caves
   - ○ D. Great Smoky Mountains

2. What makes Mammoth Caves different than the other parks?
   - ○ A. It is in the East.
   - ○ B. It is beautiful.
   - ○ C. It's underground.
   - ○ D. It has park rangers.

# ☺ BrainTeaser ☺

The starting letters in all the two-word phrases below are missing. The remaining letters, while *in order*, are pushed together. Both words in the phrase start with the same letter. Decide which letter is missing from each two-word phrase, then rewrite the phrase. The first one is done for you.

1. u m b o e t _____jumbo jet_____

2. a r r o t a k e _____

3. a s t a u g h _____

4. o u n d o b i n _____

5. i e d i p e r _____

6. i l d e s t _____

7. a s t o o d _____

8. t o p i g n _____

9. e a n a g _____

10. o o d r i e f _____

*Morning Jumpstarts: Reading, Grade 5* © 2013 Scholastic Teaching Resources

Name _____ Date _____

## WORD of the Day

Use the word below in a short paragraph about someone or something that affected you strongly.

**impressive:** (adj.) *able to have a strong effect on someone's mind, feelings, or conscience*

_____

_____

_____

## Sentence Mender

Rewrite the sentence to make it correct.

It taked me a long time to ketch my first fowl ball.

_____

## Cursive Quote

Copy the quotation in cursive writing.

*Say nothing about another that you wouldn't want to hear about yourself.*

—El Salvadoran proverb

_____

_____

_____

What other proverb do you know that expresses the same idea? Write your answer in cursive on another sheet of paper.

## Analogy of the Day

Complete the analogy.

**Abundant** is to **plentiful** as _____ is to **fearful**.

○ A. bountiful     ○ B. many     ○ C. fearless     ○ D. scared

Explain how the analogy works: _____

_____

 # Ready, Set, READ!

**Read the passage. Then answer the questions.**

When you think about wagon trains taking people westward you may think that they relied heavily on horses. But to those hardy 19th-century travelers, horses were not so important. Mules were. Mules were by far the favorite pack animal for settlers of the American West.

A mule is a cross between a donkey and a horse. Farmers have been breeding mules since ancient times. They, not camels, were the favorite pack animals of desert-crossing merchants centuries ago.

George Washington bred mules here in America. He understood their value to farmers. Mules could not only plow the fields, but harvest them, too. They could haul crops to market.

Mules were essential to the pioneers. Mule-drawn wagons could cover as many as 30 miles a day. That was five times as far as horses could take them! On flat, dry land, a large mule pulling a stagecoach could cover up to ten miles in an hour. That was very fast for that time. And when the travelers reached their destinations, mules were useful again. They could haul the logs needed to build new cabins.

Here's to the mule—an unsung American hero.

1. Why were mules more useful than horses to pioneers? _____

_____

2. What does it mean to be an *unsung hero*? _____

_____

# ☺ BrainTeaser ☺

Use the clues to fill in the grid with only four different words.
The word that goes in the first row also goes in the first column.
The word that goes in the second row also goes in the second column, and so on. Choose their order carefully.

**Clues:**

- cloth shelter _____

- small biting insect _____

- last word of a prayer _____

- what someone is called _____

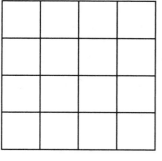

*Morning Jumpstarts: Reading, Grade 5* © 2013 Scholastic Teaching Resources

Name _____ Date _____

## WORD of the Day

Use the word below in a short paragraph about a one-sided competition or sporting event you've seen.

**overwhelm:** (v.) *overcome completely; make helpless*

_____

_____

_____

## Sentence Mender

Rewrite the sentence to make it correct.

1 of our friends Teresa lost their house keys during the buss trip.

_____

## Cursive Quote

Copy the quotation in cursive writing.

*The beautiful thing about learning is that no one can take it away from you.*

—B. B. King

_____

_____

_____

What is something else that is beautiful for the same reason? Write your answer in cursive on another sheet of paper.

## Analogy of the Day

Complete the analogy.

**Leg** is to **limb** as _____ is to **tool.**

○ A. fix      ○ B. carpenter      ○ C. shed      ○ D. pliers

Explain how the analogy works: _____

_____

## 📖 Ready, Set, READ!

Read the letter to the editor. Then answer the questions.

Dear Editor,

I am in fifth grade. I am lucky because we are learning to speak Chinese in our class. I think it is so important to learn a language that many people in the world speak. I already speak English. I plan to learn to speak Spanish, too.

With everyone today using social media and the Internet, the world has become much smaller than it used to be. When something important happens anywhere, the whole world can know about it almost right away. Also, people travel a lot now. They enjoy each other's food, art, and music. People from different lands work together more than ever. They go to schools together, too.

So I believe that American students should learn a foreign language when they are young. And then they should learn another. The more we can understand our neighbors' ways and beliefs, the better we can all get along. What better way is there to know them than to speak with them?

Ari Sofer

1. What does Ari think all young students should do? Why?

_____

_____

_____

2. What do you think 謝謝 means?

_____

_____

_____

## 🌀 BrainTeaser 🌀

In each sentence below, find and cross out the extra word.

1. Anyone who is arrives late will miss out on the trip.

2. How long hand must the report be?

3. Can you help me assemble my old new skateboard?

4. Please have a parent or guardian sign in the permission slip.

5. The juggler can balance beam and toss five clubs at once.

**98**

Name _____ Date _____

## WORD of the Day

Use the word below in a short paragraph about your views on how to treat visitors to your home, school, or country.

**hospitality:** (n.) *the generous treatment of guests or strangers*

_____

_____

## Sentence Mender

**Rewrite the sentence to make it correct.**

My indian classmates' speak english and hindi.

_____

## Cursive Quote

**Copy the quotation in cursive writing.**

*Education is the ability to listen to almost anything without losing your temper.*

—Robert Frost

How do you define education? Write your answer in cursive on another sheet of paper.

## Analogy of the Day

**Complete the analogy.**

**Actor** is to **cast** as _____ is to **state**.

O A. city     O B. country     O C. happiness     O D. desert

Explain how the analogy works: _____

_____

# 📖 Ready, Set, READ!

**Read the story. Then answer the questions.**

You have read about the awesome feats of the logger Paul Bunyan and his giant blue ox, Babe. But the story of his earliest years is less well known.

Paul was born in Maine. He was already so darn large that it took five giant storks to deliver him. He was such a huge baby that his crib was a lumber wagon. When he fussed at night, his howling was so loud that it sent all of Maine's fish swimming to safety in other states.

And boy, could that infant chow down! His folks had to keep 24 cows on hand just to get him enough milk each day. The ten barrels of oatmeal they fed him each morning were barely enough to keep him from starving. Would you say this kid was a handful?

Then, when Paul was about a month old, he rolled over in his sleep. That was not such a good idea. He destroyed 11 square miles of prime timberland. Well, Maine had had enough. It was too small a place for this ample youngster. So the Bunyans packed up and moved west to Minnesota, where he might fit. And that is where Paul Bunyan truly became larger than life.

1. Why did Paul's family move west?
   - ○ A. He howled too much.
   - ○ B. He rolled over in his sleep.
   - ○ C. He drank too much milk.
   - ○ D. He broke his crib.

2. Which best describes young Paul?
   - ○ A. restless
   - ○ B. loud
   - ○ C. enormous
   - ○ D. hungry

# 🌀 BrainTeaser 🌀

**Write the missing word for each expression.**

1. trial and _____

2. hit or _____

3. rough and _____

4. bird's-eye _____

5. haste makes _____

6. _____ and shine

7. _____ on wood

8. _____ a leg

9. _____ over heels

10. _____ or wrong

Morning Jumpstarts: Reading, Grade 5 © 2013 Scholastic Teaching Resources

Name _____ Date _____

## WORD of the Day

Use the word below in a short paragraph about a time you worked very hard on something.

**industrious**: (adj.) *working hard and steadily; diligent*

_____

_____

_____

## Sentence Mender

**Rewrite the sentence to make it correct.**

my brother doe'snt swim as fast as me can

_____

## Cursive Quote

**Copy the quotation in cursive writing.**

*If you like things easy, you'll have difficulties; if you like problems, you'll succeed.*

—Laotian proverb

_____

_____

_____

**Do you agree? Explain. Write your answer in cursive on another sheet of paper.**

## Analogy of the Day

**Complete the analogy.**

**Engine** is to **truck** as _____ is to **camera**.

○ A. photographer     ○ B. photograph     ○ C. lens     ○ D. digital

Explain how the analogy works: _____

_____

## 📖 Ready, Set, READ!

**Read the passage. Then answer the questions.**

People are lined up early along Brooklyn's Eastern Parkway. There are more than a million of them. It's the first Monday in September and they are waiting for the start of New York's largest and loudest street festival. It's Labor Day—time for the annual West Indian–American Day Parade.

The flags of Caribbean nations are flying. People are dancing to soca, calypso, reggae, ska, and compas music played by the many steel bands. The aroma of regional specialties like Jamaican jerk chicken and Bajan fried flying fish fills the air. The parade floats are built and ready using this year's themes. The masqueraders are in place. And here they come.

There are thousands of people dressed in ornate costumes with vibrant colors. The elaborate floats are incredible. They're packed with revelers jumping up and down. The pageantry is amazing. The noise is deafening but enticing. The onlookers are exhilarated. They are waving and singing. The excitement is the once-a-year kind.

1. On what national holiday does the parade occur?

_____

_____

2. Based on the passage, what do you think a *masquerader* is? _____

_____

## ๑ BrainTeaser ๑

This word link uses colors:

   yellow → white → eggshell → lavender

**Link words by starting a new word with the *last* letter of the word before. How long a word link can you make? Continue the link of state names started below.**

Ohio → Oregon → _____

_____

_____

_____

*Morning Jumpstarts: Reading, Grade 5* © 2013 Scholastic Teaching Resources

Name _____ Date _____

## WORD of the Day

Use the word below in a short paragraph about something you value highly and of which you take special care.

**cherish**: (v.) *treat tenderly, lovingly, and carefully*

_____

_____

_____

## Sentence Mender

Rewrite the sentence to make it correct.

Grady and Rob is the too host's of the partay.

_____

## Cursive Quote

Copy the quotation in cursive writing.

*Reading takes us away from home, but more important, it finds homes for us everywhere.*          —Hazel Rochman

.................................................

.................................................

.................................................

What do you think this means? Write your answer in cursive on another sheet of paper.

## Analogy of the Day

Complete the analogy.

**Warm** is to **sizzling** as _____ is to **exhausted**.

○ A. awake     ○ B. peppy     ○ C. weary     ○ D. boiling

Explain how the analogy works: _____

_____

 # Ready, Set, READ!

**Read the passage. Then answer the questions.**

I am not a fan of mayonnaise. But millions are. They slab it on sandwiches and put it in egg salad. Some even enjoy it on their burgers. Yecch. And what would a BLT be without it? "Mayo" is an everyday part of our food life.

This common condiment was first made on the Spanish island of Minorca in 1756. It was a sauce made from raw egg yolk, olive oil, and lemon juice. It was created by the personal chef of a visiting French duke. When the duke went back home, he brought the condiment with him. It took on the name of the port where he first landed: Mahon. Mahon sauce added flavor to meats. The French loved it!

Mayonnaise (the French spelling) arrived in America a century later. For years it was considered too hard for most cooks to make at home. But the arrival of the electric blender and the plans of Richard Hellman spread the mayonnaise far and wide! That resourceful deli owner began to bottle his own version of it. He put it in large jars with blue ribbons on each one. Then he began to sell it. That's how a once-exotic condiment meant for a royal feast became, well, mayo.

1. Where was mayonnaise first made?

_____

_____

_____

_____

_____

2. Why did it take so long for mayo to become a popular condiment?

_____

_____

_____

_____

_____

_____

## ✎ BrainTeaser ✎

The table gives two sets of three-letter words. Pick one word from each column to form a new six-letter word.

| Column 1 | Column 2 | New six-letter word |
|----------|----------|---------------------|
| bit | did | |
| but | her | |
| can | ice | |
| off | per | |
| pup | pet | |
| rat | red | |
| sac | ten | |
| zip | ton | |

Name _____ Date _____

## WORD of the Day

Use the word below in a short paragraph about a legend you find fascinating.

**myth:** (n.) *a legend or old story, usually one that tries to explain how something came to be*

_____

_____

_____

## Sentence Mender

**Rewrite the sentence to make it correct.**

Nikos dad really nose the rope when it come to sayling.

_____

## Cursive Quote

**Copy the quotation in cursive writing.**

*Tell me and I'll forget, show me and I may not remember. Involve me, and I'll understand.* —Native American saying

_____

_____

How do you learn best? Explain. Write your answer in cursive on another sheet of paper.

## Analogy of the Day

**Complete the analogy.**

**High** is to **low** as _____ is to **bored**.

○ A. zero    ○ B. wood    ○ C. board    ○ D. interested

Explain how the analogy works: _____

_____

## 📖 Ready, Set, READ!

**Read the passage. Then answer the questions.**

American children's author Jean Fritz spent her childhood in China. From that great distance, she developed a passion for American history. In her books she writes about famous Americans. She writes in a way that describes her subjects as real people. She explains what they were truly like. She tries to put into plain words why they did what they did. She brings them to life.

She wrote about what Paul Revere felt and thought as he played his part in the fight for independence. She wrote about why John Hancock always sought the approval of others. She clarified why Benedict Arnold chose to betray his country. She always put great effort into her research. She tried to know her subjects as well as their friends and family did.

When she gives advice to children who want to write, Fritz recommends that they keep journals. She encourages them to write not only about events, but about feelings they are having. She guides them to write what's inside them, not what they think their teachers or parents want to read.

1. What does Jean Fritz think is essential to put in her books?

_____

_____

_____

_____

_____

_____

2. What is your take on the advice Fritz gives to young writers?

_____

_____

_____

_____

_____

_____

## ☺ BrainTeaser ☺

Long ago, people sent critical messages by telegram.
Senders paid by the word, so they attempted to be brief and clear.
(Punctuation was free. Add it where it's needed.)

**Use each of the letters below to start the words of a telegram giving valuable information.**

W_____  R_____  D_____  S_____

P_____  L_____  H_____  N_____

Morning Jumpstarts: Reading, Grade 5 © 2013 Scholastic Teaching Resources

Name _____ Date _____

**WORD of the Day**

Use the word below in a short paragraph describing a fancy, elegant place.

**luxurious:** (adj.) *very comfortable and beautiful*

_____
_____
_____

## Sentence Mender

**Rewrite the sentence to make it correct.**

I told my gramother about the tornadoe that hits last weak.

_____

## Cursive Quote

**Copy the quotation in cursive writing.**

*You're not obligated to win. You're obligated to keep trying to do the best you can every day.*
—Marian Wright Edelman

What do you think about this advice? Write your answer in cursive on another sheet of paper.

## Analogy of the Day

**Complete the analogy.**

**Improvement** is to **practice** as _____ is to **fertilize**.

○ A. growth    ○ B. plant    ○ C. multiply    ○ D. farm

Explain how the analogy works: _____
_____

## 📖 Ready, Set, READ!

**Read the passage. Then answer the questions.**

The potato is a starchy vegetable with a thin skin. It is the most common carbohydrate in the American diet. And it is misunderstood.

The potato is not a food the Europeans brought to the Americas. Rather, it was something the European explorers brought back *from* the Americas with them. Potatoes were first grown in the Andes in South America. There are about 5,000 varieties of potatoes worldwide.

Now to the misunderstood part. Suppose you were on a diet and had to choose between a 5-ounce baked potato and a 5-ounce steak. You may not want to choose the meat. It has five times the number of calories a potato does! The potato is not fattening. And it is a terrific source of the vitamins and minerals we need for growth and health. If we eat the skin too, the potato is a nearly sufficient diet all by itself. For instance, it provides 45% of our daily need of vitamin C. And its skin has as much fiber as cereal or whole grain bread does.

So, if you can avoid slathering butter or sour cream on your spud, your kidneys, intestines, stomach, and doctor will be happy. Eat a plain potato if you wish!

1. Where did potatoes come from? _____

_____

2. Why are potatoes misunderstood? _____

_____

3. What do you think a *spud* is? _____

_____

## 🌀 BrainTeaser 🌀

Write a funny meaning for each of the totally made-up words below.
The first one will give you the idea.

1. snorzabaga   _sleeping bag for a noisy sleeper_ _____

2. clabbing    _____

3. disjulled    _____

4. overglitch    _____

5. requimble    _____

*Morning Jumpstarts: Reading, Grade 5* © 2013 Scholastic Teaching Resources

# Answers

## Jumpstart 1
**Word of the Day:** Check students' paragraphs for accurate usage of the term.
**Sentence Mender:** "I won first prize," Kerry said with pride.
**Cursive Quote:** Check students' handwriting for accuracy and legibility. Responses will vary.
**Analogy of the Day:** D; (object-location analogy) Check that students' answers are reasonable.
**Ready, Set, Read! 1.** He means that he knows what he's talking about. **2.** Molly seemed frustrated that her owner did not understand what she wanted.
**Brainteaser:** Answers may vary; sample answer: hive, have, cave, cake

## Jumpstart 2
**Word of the Day:** Check students' paragraphs for accurate usage of the term.
**Sentence Mender:** Jason's bruise on his leg caused him to limp.
**Cursive Quote:** Check students' handwriting for accuracy and legibility. Responses will vary.
**Analogy of the Day:** B; (antonyms analogy) Check that students' answers are reasonable.
**Ready, Set, Read! 1.** The writer means that the spicy peppers felt burning hot.
**2.** That's a low Scoville number, so the pepper would taste mild.
**Brainteaser: 1.** patty **2.** patch **3.** patio **4.** patrol **5.** pattern **6.** patient

## Jumpstart 3
**Word of the Day:** Check students' paragraphs for accurate usage of the term.
**Sentence Mender:** The new glass building on Spring Street sparkles like a diamond.
**Cursive Quote:** Check students' handwriting for accuracy and legibility. Responses will vary.
**Analogy of the Day:** C; (cause-and-effect analogy) Check that students' answers are reasonable.
**Ready, Set, Read! 1.** They were honest men who didn't want to hurt their good reputation. **2.** It means spoke highly of them and their work to other people. **3.** Mano and Miklos come to America and start a successful painting business.
**Brainteaser:** (Top to bottom) sobbed, soccer, sonata, sorrow, sortie, spider; drawer

## Jumpstart 4
**Word of the Day:** Check students' paragraphs for accurate usage of the term.
**Sentence Mender:** We should ask him to cease playing his drums so late at night.
**Cursive Quote:** Check students' handwriting for accuracy and legibility. Responses will vary.
**Analogy of the Day:** A; (sequence analogy) Check that students' answers are reasonable.
**Ready, Set, Read! 1.** They left to get away from hostile neighbors. **2.** B
**Brainteaser: 1.** race/care **2.** step/pets **3.** blade **4.** cater/trace **5.** prays/spray **6.** mopes

## Jumpstart 5
**Word of the Day:** Check students' paragraphs for accurate usage of the term.
**Sentence Mender:** The Detroit Tigers played a doubleheader on Labor Day.
**Cursive Quote:** Check students' handwriting for accuracy and legibility. Responses will vary.
**Analogy of the Day:** D; (class-example relationship analogy) Check that students' answers are reasonable.
**Ready, Set, Read! 1.** It means that it got his attention. **2.** Both were first known only by their fossil records.
**Brainteaser:** Answers may vary; sample answer: If Stu chews short shoes, should Stu choose the short shoes he chews?

## Jumpstart 6
**Word of the Day:** Check students' paragraphs for accurate usage of the term.
**Sentence Mender:** What is the height, in feet, of that eight-story building?
**Cursive Quote:** Check students' handwriting for accuracy and legibility. Responses will vary.
**Analogy of the Day:** B; (object-description relationship analogy) Check that students' answers are reasonable.
**Ready, Set, Read! 1.** D **2.** C
**Brainteaser:** Answers will vary; sample answers: **1.** clatter **2.** tick **3.** burble **4.** trudge **5.** rattle **6.** hoot

## Jumpstart 7
**Word of the Day:** Check students' paragraphs for accurate usage of the term.
**Sentence Mender:** The determined inventor would not concede defeat.
**Cursive Quote:** Check students' handwriting for accuracy and legibility. Responses will vary.
**Analogy of the Day:** B; (part-whole analogy) Check that students' answers are reasonable.
**Ready, Set, Read! 1.** A rumpus is a noisy disturbance. **2.** Pete was dreaming.
**Brainteaser: 1.** level **2.** sexes **3.** refer **4.** redder **5.** solos

## Jumpstart 8
**Word of the Day:** Check students' paragraphs for accurate usage of the term.
**Sentence Mender:** He's the oldest and biggest of the three brothers.
**Cursive Quote:** Check students' handwriting for accuracy and legibility. Responses will vary.
**Analogy of the Day:** D; (member-group analogy) Check that students' answers are reasonable.
**Ready, Set, Read! 1.** You can go to the International Space Station or take a suborbital flight. **2.** The writer implies that the prices are actually very high.
**Brainteaser: 1.** gray day **2.** flag bag **3.** claw flaw **4.** broom room **5.** flight fright

## Jumpstart 9
**Word of the Day:** Check students' paragraphs for accurate usage of the term.
**Sentence Mender:** The park ranger led us on the descent from the mountain.
**Cursive Quote:** Check students' handwriting for accuracy and legibility. Responses will vary.
**Analogy of the Day:** C; (degree of meaning analogy) Check that students' answers are reasonable.
**Ready, Set, Read! 1.** A feeder is a river that empties into another. **2.** Answers will vary; sample answer: It is the largest and best known waterway in North America.
**Brainteaser: 1.** cracker packer **2.** stable fable **3.** limber timber **4.** critter sitter **5.** clipper skipper

## Jumpstart 10
**Word of the Day:** Check students' paragraphs for accurate usage of the term.
**Sentence Mender:** Dan and Iris went to Paris to take a French cooking class.
**Cursive Quote:** Check students' handwriting for accuracy and legibility. Responses will vary.
**Analogy of the Day:** B; (antonyms analogy) Check that students' answers are reasonable.
**Ready, Set, Read! 1.** The writer means that the two styles of dance worked well together. **2.** Juba is a traditional African dance form.
**Brainteaser:** (Top to bottom) blend, theft, hairy, amaze, brood; zebra

## Jumpstart 11
**Word of the Day:** Check students' paragraphs for accurate usage of the term.
**Sentence Mender:** We visited South Carolina's first lighthouse.
**Cursive Quote:** Check students' handwriting for accuracy and legibility. Responses will vary.
**Analogy of the Day:** A; (object-action analogy) Check that students' answers are reasonable.
**Ready, Set, Read! 1.** C **2.** A
**Brainteaser:**

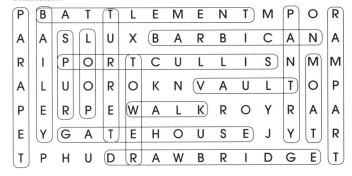

## Jumpstart 12
**Word of the Day:** Check students' paragraphs for accurate usage of the term.
**Sentence Mender:** This morning, I had breakfast in my pajamas and spilled orange juice on them.
**Cursive Quote:** Check students' handwriting for accuracy and legibility. Responses will vary.
**Analogy of the Day:** A; (example-class analogy) Check that students' answers are reasonable.
**Ready, Set, Read! 1.** They thought it was only sparsely inhabited. **2.** It tells us that a rich and populous culture once existed in the area.
**Brainteaser: 1.** mourn **2.** omit **3.** duplicate **4.** support **5.** attack **6.** impartial **7.** barrier

## Jumpstart 13

**Word of the Day:** Check students' paragraphs for accurate usage of the term.
**Sentence Mender:** What should we do about the worrisome leak in the kitchen?
**Cursive Quote:** Check students' handwriting for accuracy and legibility. Responses will vary.
**Analogy of the Day:** D; (object-description analogy) Check that students' answers are reasonable.
**Ready, Set, Read! 1.** Huge lines, geometric shapes, and animal figures were scraped into the ground. **2.** Scientists suggest that the Nazca people built them to please their gods.
**Brainteaser: 2.** hate, heat **3.** huts, shut **4.** race, acre **5.** swear, wears

## Jumpstart 14

**Word of the Day:** Check students' paragraphs for accurate usage of the term.
**Sentence Mender:** The number has two sixes and three fours.
**Cursive Quote:** Check students' handwriting for accuracy and legibility. Responses will vary.
**Analogy of the Day:** B; (object-location analogy) Check that students' answers are reasonable.
**Ready, Set, Read! 1.** The Cardiff Giant was buried there. **2.** This statement suggests that people can be easily fooled.
**Brainteaser:**

| Word | 1 thing | 2 or more | Can't tell |
|---|---|---|---|
| 1. furniture | | | ✓ |
| 2. aircraft | | | ✓ |
| 3. oxen | | ✓ | |
| 4. moose | | | ✓ |
| 5. dice | | ✓ | |
| 6. cactus | ✓ | | |
| 7. people | | ✓ | |

## Jumpstart 15

**Word of the Day:** Check students' paragraphs for accurate usage of the term.
**Sentence Mender:** Meg's teacher and her mom agree that Meg's handwriting is illegible.
**Cursive Quote:** Check students' handwriting for accuracy and legibility. Responses will vary.
**Analogy of the Day:** A; (cause-and-effect analogy) Check that students' answers are reasonable.
**Ready, Set, Read! 1.** She wrote about wilderness and wildlife. **2.** She grew up in a family that appreciated nature in all forms.
**Brainteaser: 1.** Texas **2.** Vermont **3.** Kentucky **4.** Nebraska **5.** Wisconsin **6.** Delaware **7.** Maryland **8.** Florida **9.** Kansas **10.** Montana

## Jumpstart 16

**Word of the Day:** Check students' paragraphs for accurate usage of the term.
**Sentence Mender:** It is easier to put a bridle on a horse than on a mule.
**Cursive Quote:** Check students' handwriting for accuracy and legibility. Responses will vary.
**Analogy of the Day:** D; (part-whole analogy) Check that students' answers are reasonable.
**Ready, Set, Read! 1.** C **2.** A
**Brainteaser:** Answers will vary; sample answer:

| | F | A | C | T |
|---|---|---|---|---|
| Cars | Ford | Audi | Cadillac | Toyota |
| Colors | forest green | apricot | cobalt | tan |
| Foods | fish | apple | carrots | taco |
| Languages | French | Arabic | Chinese | Turkish |

## Jumpstart 17

**Word of the Day:** Check students' paragraphs for accurate usage of the term.
**Sentence Mender:** The track team's captain can run like a deer.
**Cursive Quote:** Check students' handwriting for accuracy and legibility. Responses will vary.
**Analogy of the Day:** D; (member-group analogy) Check that students' answers are reasonable.
**Ready, Set, Read! 1.** Their task was to map the Pacific Ocean. **2.** Wilkes discovered that Antarctica was a continent, and greatly increased our knowledge of the world.
**Brainteaser: 1.** zoo **2.** you **3.** tutu **4.** knew **5.** clue **6.** shoe **7.** view **8.** Peru

## Jumpstart 18

**Word of the Day:** Check students' paragraphs for accurate usage of the term..
**Sentence Mender:** That wonderful dog Gracie is the apple of her owner's eye.
**Cursive Quote:** Check students' handwriting for accuracy and legibility. Responses will vary.
**Analogy of the Day:** B; (object-action analogy) Check that students' answers are reasonable.
**Ready, Set, Read! 1.** The Methuselah is about 2,100 years older. **2.** The Hyperion tree is 380 feet tall. **3.** Circumference is the distance around something circular.
**Brainteaser:** Answers will vary; check students' word lists.

## Jumpstart 19

**Word of the Day:** Check students' paragraphs for accurate usage of the term.
**Sentence Mender:** Many cable customers have found the new service to be worse than it was before.
**Cursive Quote:** Check students' handwriting for accuracy and legibility. Responses will vary.
**Analogy of the Day:** C; (object-function analogy) Check that students' answers are reasonable.
**Ready, Set, Read! 1.** The writer was visiting a ghost town. **2.** Answers will vary; sample answer: The ghosts of the town's past came to life. **3.** Agape means wide-open.
**Brainteaser: 1.** Close the garage door. **2.** How can you trust a liar? **3.** Noisy noises annoy oysters. **4.** They haven't yet eaten lunch. **5.** Are you learning to speak Spanish?

## Jumpstart 20

**Word of the Day:** Check students' paragraphs for accurate usage of the term.
**Sentence Mender:** Erin was upset when she learned that she couldn't go with her friends.
**Cursive Quote:** Check students' handwriting for accuracy and legibility. Responses will vary.
**Analogy of the Day:** B; (object-description analogy) Check that students' answers are reasonable.
**Ready, Set, Read! 1.** They were major leaders in the 19th-century women's movement. **2.** Answers will vary; sample answer: Many people disagreed with their goals.
**Brainteaser: 1.** tent **2.** tenth **3.** tenor **4.** tennis **5.** tender **6.** tenpins **7.** tension **8.** tentacle

## Jumpstart 21

**Word of the Day:** Check students' paragraphs for accurate usage of the term.
**Sentence Mender:** She was born in Troy, New York, on January 9, 2012.
**Cursive Quote:** Check students' handwriting for accuracy and legibility. Responses will vary.
**Analogy of the Day:** A; (example-class analogy) Check that students' answers are reasonable.
**Ready, Set, Read! 1.** A food writer must know a lot about food and must be a good writer. **2.** Endeavor means to try.
**Brainteaser: 1.** except **2.** passed **3.** affect **4.** stares **5.** whether **6.** guest

## Jumpstart 22

**Word of the Day:** Check students' paragraphs for accurate usage of the term.
**Sentence Mender:** Either Jack, Ilsa, or Andrew will enter a muffin recipe in the contest. Note: the series comma before *or* is optional.
**Cursive Quote:** Check students' handwriting for accuracy and legibility. Responses will vary.
**Analogy of the Day:** A; (object-description analogy) Check that students' answers are reasonable.
**Ready, Set, Read! 1.** D **2.** C
**Brainteaser:** (Top to bottom) paper, eight, daily, smash, greet; graph

## Jumpstart 23

**Word of the Day:** Check students' paragraphs for accurate usage of the term.
**Sentence Mender:** Hey! Where are you going with my cell phone?
**Cursive Quote:** Check students' handwriting for accuracy and legibility. Responses will vary.
**Analogy of the Day:** D; (synonyms analogy) Check that students' answers are reasonable.
**Ready, Set, Read! 1.** Prep time is when you gather materials and ingredients before you cook. **2.** The asterisk shows where to find added information. **3.** 20 g
**Brainteaser:** Answers will vary; sample answers: dad, pop, bib, wow; Elle, Anna, toot; kayak, madam

## Jumpstart 24

**Word of the Day:** Check students' paragraphs for accurate usage of the term.
**Sentence Mender:** The chef realized that she needed more pepper, salt, and onion in the stew. Note: the series comma before *and* is optional.
**Cursive Quote:** Check students' handwriting for accuracy and legibility. Responses will vary.
**Analogy of the Day:** C; (member-group analogy) Check that students' answers are reasonable.
**Ready, Set, Read! 1.** Their best player was injured and couldn't play. **2.** He could barely walk, but he led his team to a championship by hitting a home run on demand.
**Brainteaser: 1.** reject **2.** mild **3.** flee **4.** lose **5.** merciful **6.** sensible **7.** feast **8.** sluggish

*Morning Jumpstarts: Reading, Grade 5* © 2013 Scholastic Teaching Resources

## Jumpstart 25
**Word of the Day:** Check students' paragraphs for accurate usage of the term.
**Sentence Mender:** I finally got to play for the maestro, but he wasn't impressed with my effort.
**Cursive Quote:** Check students' handwriting for accuracy and legibility. Responses will vary.
**Analogy of the Day:** B; (object-function analogy) Check that students' answers are reasonable.
**Ready, Set, Read!** Questions will vary; sample questions: **1.** How many dentists were asked? **2.** What exactly does being the #1 toothpaste refer to? **3.** Who cares about getting a toothpaste poster?
**Brainteaser:** Answers will vary; sample answers: honeyed/harsh, candied/tart; wonderful/awful, excellent/poor, terrific/terrible

## Jumpstart 26
**Word of the Day:** Check students' paragraphs for accurate usage of the term.
**Sentence Mender:** After tripping on a gopher hole in the pasture, she could hardly walk.
**Cursive Quote:** Check students' handwriting for accuracy and legibility. Responses will vary.
**Analogy of the Day:** D; (antonyms analogy) Check that students' answers are reasonable.
**Ready, Set, Read! 1.** D **2.** B
**Brainteaser: 1.** ox **2.** mix **3.** apex **4.** jinx **5.** coax **6.** relax **7.** index **8.** earwax

## Jumpstart 27
**Word of the Day:** Check students' paragraphs for accurate usage of the term.
**Sentence Mender:** The singer now has won an Oscar and a Grammy award.
**Cursive Quote:** Check students' handwriting for accuracy and legibility. Responses will vary.
**Analogy of the Day:** B; (sequence analogy) Check that students' answers are reasonable.
**Ready, Set, Read! 1.** They can teach lessons about right and wrong. **2.** Genre is a kind or style of writing.
**Brainteaser: 1.** bullpen **2.** shortstop **3.** double **4.** umpire **5.** dugout **6.** backstop **7.** infield **8.** bleachers **9.** manager **10.** rookie

## Jumpstart 28
**Word of the Day:** Check students' paragraphs for accurate usage of the term.
**Sentence Mender:** Both she and Nina missed the science test.
**Cursive Quote:** Check students' handwriting for accuracy and legibility. Responses will vary.
**Analogy of the Day:** C; (object-location analogy) Check that students' answers are reasonable.
**Ready, Set, Read! 1.** It means to live peacefully with neighbors and the surroundings. **2.** The plants offered the humans sources of medicine.
**Brainteaser:** (Top to bottom) rain, tie, cancel; an electrician

## Jumpstart 29
**Word of the Day:** Check students' paragraphs for accurate usage of the term.
**Sentence Mender:** Miguel told Victor that he didn't need to practice anymore.
**Cursive Quote:** Check students' handwriting for accuracy and legibility. Responses will vary.
**Analogy of the Day:** A; (part-whole analogy) Check that students' answers are reasonable.
**Ready, Set, Read! 1.** C **2.** D **3.** C
**Brainteaser: 2.** cap **3.** tank **4.** plate **5.** oil **6.** cheese

## Jumpstart 30
**Word of the Day:** Check students' paragraphs for accurate usage of the term.
**Sentence Mender:** First he poured the cereal and then he added fruit and milk.
**Cursive Quote:** Check students' handwriting for accuracy and legibility. Responses will vary.
**Analogy of the Day:** D; (object-user analogy) Check that students' answers are reasonable.
**Ready, Set, Read! 1.** They wanted to glorify the American landscape. **2.** It means that you are awestruck. **3.** You can see it online.
**Brainteaser: 1.** able, bale **2.** blow, bowl **3.** tools, stool **4.** rinse, risen **5.** dopes, posed

## Jumpstart 31
**Word of the Day:** Check students' paragraphs for accurate usage of the term.
**Sentence Mender:** Many people get sick from mosquito bites.
**Cursive Quote:** Check students' handwriting for accuracy and legibility. Responses will vary.
**Analogy of the Day:** C; (cause-and-effect analogy) Check that students' answers are reasonable.
**Ready, Set, Read! 1.** The Creeks left to get away from warring tribes. **2.** The U. S. Army was unable to subdue them or get them to do what it wanted.
**Brainteaser:** Answers will vary; check students' adjectives.

## Jumpstart 32
**Word of the Day:** Check students' paragraphs for accurate usage of the term.
**Sentence Mender:** Before Labor Day, we were happy and everything seemed perfect.
**Cursive Quote:** Check students' handwriting for accuracy and legibility. Responses will vary.
**Analogy of the Day:** B; (example-class analogy) Check that students' answers are reasonable.
**Ready, Set, Read! 1.** He was the first American to try to make a living as a full-time songwriter. **2.** It suggests that life as an artist is not easy.
**Brainteaser:** Answers will vary; check students' verbs.

## Jumpstart 33
**Word of the Day:** Check students' paragraphs for accurate usage of the term.
**Sentence Mender:** "There are bear tracks ahead on the trail, so be careful," the ranger warned.
**Cursive Quote:** Check students' handwriting for accuracy and legibility. Responses will vary.
**Analogy of the Day:** A; (antonyms analogy) Check that students' answers are reasonable.
**Ready, Set, Read! 1.** She saw the Wright Brothers' first flight. **2.** Answers will vary; sample answer: She was using e-mail long before it was invented.
**Brainteaser:** Answers will vary; sample answer: The trumpet teacher took ten talkative teens to task today.

## Jumpstart 34
**Word of the Day:** Check students' paragraphs for accurate usage of the term.
**Sentence Mender:** Henry wondered who won the World Series last year.
**Cursive Quote:** Check students' handwriting for accuracy and legibility. Responses will vary.
**Analogy of the Day:** B; (degree of meaning or synonyms analogy) Check that students' answers are reasonable.
**Ready, Set, Read! 1.** B **2.** C **3.** D
**Brainteaser:** Answers may vary; sample answer: husk, hulk, hull, bull, bell

## Jumpstart 35
**Word of the Day:** Check students' paragraphs for accurate usage of the term.
**Sentence Mender:** I read an article called "How to Join Social Networks."
**Cursive Quote:** Check students' handwriting for accuracy and legibility. Responses will vary.
**Analogy of the Day:** B; (synonyms analogy) Check that students' answers are reasonable.
**Ready, Set, Read! 1.** It means that the poet is not exaggerating. **2.** Answers will vary; sample answer: I think the poet may have had this kind of experience with a dog. **3.** He means that it's just like a soaking-wet dog to make contact with its owner.
**Brainteaser:** (Top to bottom) 4, 5, 3, 7, 6, 1, 2

## Jumpstart 36
**Word of the Day:** Check students' paragraphs for accurate usage of the term.
**Sentence Mender:** The Empire State Building is taller than the Chrysler Building.
**Cursive Quote:** Check students' handwriting for accuracy and legibility. Responses will vary.
**Analogy of the Day:** C; (member-group analogy) Check that students' answers are reasonable.
**Ready, Set, Read! 1.** A **2.** B **3.** Answers will vary; sample answer: She has experience with large dogs.
**Brainteaser:** (Top to bottom) cursor, van, week; a nervous wreck

## Jumpstart 37
**Word of the Day:** Check students' paragraphs for accurate usage of the term.
**Sentence Mender:** Matt Clark opened the door and stepped out.
**Cursive Quote:** Check students' handwriting for accuracy and legibility. Responses will vary.
**Analogy of the Day:** D; (part-whole analogy) Check that students' answers are reasonable.
**Ready, Set, Read! 1.** The reviewer finds this movie laughably bad. **2.** Answers will vary; sample answer: The tone includes sarcasm, such as "monster so unscary that you want to take it home and cuddle it."
**Brainteaser:** Answers will vary; check students' word lists.

## Jumpstart 38
**Word of the Day:** Check students' paragraphs for accurate usage of the term.
**Sentence Mender:** The knight showed his bravery in battle and was rewarded with land and a title.
**Cursive Quote:** Check students' handwriting for accuracy and legibility. Responses will vary.
**Analogy of the Day:** C; (object-description analogy) Check that students' answers are reasonable.
**Ready, Set, Read! 1.** He was a drummer boy for a Michigan regiment. **2.** He was so very young.
**Brainteaser:** (Top to bottom) Ed, red, deer, deter, rented, retuned, dentures

## Jumpstart 39
**Word of the Day:** Check students' paragraphs for accurate usage of the term.
**Sentence Mender:** "We're going to the zoo when the new monkeys arrive," said Max's sister.
**Cursive Quote:** Check students' handwriting for accuracy and legibility. Responses will vary.
**Analogy of the Day:** D; (antonyms analogy) Check that students' answers are reasonable.
**Ready, Set, Read! 1.** There is a rebellion. **2.** Answers will vary; sample answer: He is against the rebels, because he says "we'll make them flee." **3.** It means that it's too late for peaceful solutions.
**Brainteaser:**

```
S O A P T B A R I T O N E
O C R E E L H B U G O T
P L T N A T Y A N K T L
R E S T O T R E K E Y
A F L F R Y C H O R D S R
N U C L H A R M O N Y N I
O C T A V E W S H A R P C
D R E T E M P O K B A S S
```

## Jumpstart 40
**Word of the Day:** Check students' paragraphs for accurate usage of the term.
**Sentence Mender:** It used to be that few college graduates lived with their parents.
**Cursive Quote:** Check students' handwriting for accuracy and legibility. Responses will vary.
**Analogy of the Day:** A; (object-function analogy) Check that students' answers are reasonable.
**Ready, Set, Read! 1.** All the foods are wrapped inside some form of bread or pastry. **2.** They differ in the kinds of fillings and wraps.
**Brainteaser: 1.** hillbilly **2.** football **3.** address **4.** sweetness **5.** goddess **6.** coffee **7.** raccoon **8.** dumbbell

## Jumpstart 41
**Word of the Day:** Check students' paragraphs for accurate usage of the term.
**Sentence Mender:** Ethan, Ellis, and Eli are the best tenors in the church choir. Note: the series comma before *and* is optional.
**Cursive Quote:** Check students' handwriting for accuracy and legibility. Responses will vary.
**Analogy of the Day:** B; (object-user analogy) Check that students' answers are reasonable.
**Ready, Set, Read! 1.** Both were originally spread by word of mouth. **2.** Myths explain how the world works or came to be, while fables attempt to teach a lesson. **3.** Answers and explanations will vary.
**Brainteaser: 1.** towel or sponge **2.** a ton **3.** the wind **4.** a hole **5.** a river

## Jumpstart 42
**Word of the Day:** Check students' paragraphs for accurate usage of the term.
**Sentence Mender:** Marie Curie was a scientist who was ahead of her time.
**Cursive Quote:** Check students' handwriting for accuracy and legibility. Responses will vary.
**Analogy of the Day:** C; (object-location analogy) Check that students' answers are reasonable.
**Ready, Set, Read! 1.** He made people believe that the earth was being invaded by aliens. **2.** Today, people might look to other sources to try to confirm or deny the story. **3.** D
**Brainteaser:**

| Person's Name | Person's Job | Score (high, middle, low) |
| --- | --- | --- |
| Ava | dentist | high |
| Jorge | clerk | middle |
| Rex | baker | low |

## Jumpstart 43
**Word of the Day:** Check students' paragraphs for accurate usage of the term.
**Sentence Mender:** You and I should receive awards for spelling and grammar greatness.
**Cursive Quote:** Check students' handwriting for accuracy and legibility. Responses will vary.
**Analogy of the Day:** B; (object-function analogy) Check that students' answers are reasonable.
**Ready, Set, Read! 1.** D **2.** C
**Brainteaser: 2.** carrot cake **3.** last laugh **4.** round robin **5.** Pied Piper **6.** wild west **7.** fast food **8.** stop sign **9.** bean bag **10.** good grief

## Jumpstart 44
**Word of the Day:** Check students' paragraphs for accurate usage of the term.
**Sentence Mender:** It took me a long time to catch my first foul ball.
**Cursive Quote:** Check students' handwriting for accuracy and legibility. Responses will vary.
**Analogy of the Day:** D; (synonyms analogy) Check that students' answers are reasonable.
**Ready, Set, Read! 1.** Mules were faster and sturdier. **2.** An unsung hero gets little or no recognition or honor.
**Brainteaser:**

| g | n | a | t |
| --- | --- | --- | --- |
| n | a | m | e |
| a | m | e | n |
| t | e | n | t |

## Jumpstart 45
**Word of the Day:** Check students' paragraphs for accurate usage of the term.
**Sentence Mender:** One of our friends, Teresa, lost her house keys during the bus trip.
**Cursive Quote:** Check students' handwriting for accuracy and legibility. Responses will vary.
**Analogy of the Day:** D; (example-class analogy) Check that students' answers are reasonable.
**Ready, Set, Read! 1.** Ari thinks that all students should learn to speak at least two languages. He believes that people form better understandings when they can speak together. **2.** Answers may vary; sample answers: Thank you or Sincerely.
**Brainteaser: 1.** is **2.** hand **3.** old **4.** in **5.** beam

## Jumpstart 46
**Word of the Day:** Check students' paragraphs for accurate usage of the term.
**Sentence Mender:** My Indian classmates speak English and Hindi.
**Cursive Quote:** Check students' handwriting for accuracy and legibility. Responses will vary.
**Analogy of the Day:** A; (member-group analogy) Check that students' answers are reasonable.
**Ready, Set, Read! 1.** B **2.** C
**Brainteaser:** Answers may vary; sample answers: **1.** error **2.** miss **3.** tumble **4.** view **5.** waste **6.** rise **7.** knock **8.** break **9.** head **10.** right

## Jumpstart 47
**Word of the Day:** Check students' paragraphs for accurate usage of the term.
**Sentence Mender:** My brother doesn't swim as fast as I can.
**Cursive Quote:** Check students' handwriting for accuracy and legibility. Responses will vary.
**Analogy of the Day:** C; (part-whole analogy) Check that students' answers are reasonable.
**Ready, Set, Read! 1.** It happens on Labor Day. **2.** A masquerader is someone in a costume.
**Brainteaser:** Answers will vary; sample answers: New York, Kansas, South Dakota, Arizona, Alabama, Alaska, Arkansas, South Carolina

## Jumpstart 48
**Word of the Day:** Check students' paragraphs for accurate usage of the term.
**Sentence Mender:** Grady and Rob are the two hosts of the party.
**Cursive Quote:** Check students' handwriting for accuracy and legibility. Responses will vary.
**Analogy of the Day:** C; (degree of meaning or synonyms analogy) Check that students' answers are reasonable.
**Ready, Set, Read! 1.** Mayonnaise was first made in Minorca, Spain. **2.** It was considered too hard to make.
**Brainteaser:** Order may vary: bitten, button, candid, office, puppet, rather, sacred, zipper

## Jumpstart 49
**Word of the Day:** Check students' paragraphs for accurate usage of the term.
**Sentence Mender:** Niko's dad really knows the ropes when it comes to sailing.
**Cursive Quote:** Check students' handwriting for accuracy and legibility. Responses will vary.
**Analogy of the Day:** D; (antonyms analogy) Check that students' answers are reasonable.
**Ready, Set, Read! 1.** Fritz thinks it is essential to describe her subjects as realistic people. **2.** Answers will vary; sample answer: I think this is helpful advice.
**Brainteaser:** Answers will vary; sample telegram: Wyoming road destroyed. Seventeen people lost. Help needed.

## Jumpstart 50
**Word of the Day:** Check students' paragraphs for accurate usage of the term.
**Sentence Mender:** I told my grandmother about the tornado that hit last week.
**Cursive Quote:** Check students' handwriting for accuracy and legibility. Responses will vary.
**Analogy of the Day:** A; (cause-and-effect analogy) Check that students' answers are reasonable.
**Ready, Set, Read! 1.** Potatoes came from the Andes region of South America. **2.** Potatoes are more nutritious and less fattening than many people think. **3.** A spud is a potato.
**Brainteaser:** Answers will vary; sample answers: **2.** clapping and blabbing at the same time **3.** let out of a dull jail **4.** to make too many bad mistakes **5.** to quibble and grumble again